# An Essay on Slavery and Abolitionism

*Catharine E. Beecher*

# Contents

PREFACE. ...................................................................................................7
ESSAY ON SLAVERY AND ABOLITIONISM. .....................................8
SLAVERY IN THIS NATION. .................................................................27

# AN ESSAY ON SLAVERY AND ABOLITIONISM

BY

Catharine E. Beecher

# PREFACE.

THE following are the circumstances which occasioned the succeeding pages. A gentleman and a friend, requested the writer to assign reasons why he should not join the Abolition Society. While preparing a reply to this request, MISS GRIMKE's Address was presented, and the information communicated, of her intention to visit the North, for the purpose of using her influence among northern ladies to induce them to unite with Abolition Societies. The writer then began a private letter to Miss Grimke as a personal friend. But by the wishes and advice of others, these two efforts were finally combined in the following Essay, to be presented to the public.

The honoured and beloved name which that lady bears, so associated as it is at the South, North, and West, with all that is elegant in a scholar, refined in a gentleman, and elevated in a Christian,--the respectable sect with which she is connected,--the interesting effusions of her pen,--and her own intellectual and moral worth, must secure respect for her opinions and much personal influence. This seems to be a sufficient apology for presenting to the public some considerations in connexion with her name; considerations which may exhibit in another aspect the cause she advocates, and which it may be appropriate to consider. As such, they are respectfully commended to the public, and especially to that portion of it for which they are particularly designed.

# ESSAY ON SLAVERY AND ABOLITIONISM.

ADDRESSED TO MISS A. D. GRIMKE.

MY DEAR FRIEND,
Your public address to Christian females at the South has reached me, and I have been urged to aid in circulating it at the North. I have also been informed, that you contemplate a tour, during the ensuing year, for the purpose of exerting your influence to form Abolition Societies among ladies of the non-slave-holding States.

Our acquaintance and friendship give me a claim to your private ear; but there are reasons why it seems more desirable to address you, who now stand before the public as an advocate of Abolition measures, in a more public manner.

The object I have in view, is to present some reasons why it seems unwise and inexpedient for ladies of the non-slave-holding States to unite themselves in Abolition Societies; and thus, at the same time, to exhibit the inexpediency of the course you propose to adopt.

I would first remark, that your public address leads me to infer, that you are not sufficiently informed in regard to the feelings and opinions of Christian females at the North. Your remarks seem to assume, that the *principles* held by Abolitionists on the subject of slavery, are peculiar to them, and are not generally adopted by those at the North who oppose their *measures*. In this you are not correctly informed. In the sense in which Abolitionists explain the terms they employ, there is little, if any, difference between them and most northern persons. Especially is this true of northern persons of religious principles. I know not where to look for northern Christians, who would deny that every slave-holder is bound to treat his slaves exactly as he would claim that his own children ought to be treated in similar circumstances; that the holding of our fellow men as property, or the withholding any of the rights of freedom, for mere purposes of gain, is a sin, and ought to be immediately abandoned; and that where the laws are such, that a slave-holder cannot *legally* emancipate his slaves, without throwing them into worse bondage, he is bound to use all his influence to alter those laws, and, in the meantime, to treat his slaves, as nearly as he can, *as if* they were free.

I do not suppose there is one person in a thousand, at the North, who would dissent from these principles. They would only differ in the use of terms, and call this the doctrine of *gradual emancipation*, while Abolitionists would call it the doctrine of *immediate emancipation*.

As this is the state of public opinion at the North, there is no necessity for using any influence with northern ladies, in order that they may adopt your *principles* on the subject of slavery; for they hold them in common with yourself, and it would seem unwise, and might prove irritating, to approach them as if they held opposite sentiments.

In regard to the duty of making efforts to bring the people of the Southern States to adopt these principles, and act on them, it is entirely another matter. On this point you would find a large majority opposed to your views. Most persons in the non-slave-holding States have considered the matter of Southern slavery, as one in which they were no more called to interfere, than in the abolition of the press-gang system in England, or the tythe system of Ireland. Public opinion may have been wrong on this point, and yet have been right on all those great principles of rectitude and justice relating to slavery, which Abolitionists claim as their *distinctive* peculiarities.

The distinctive peculiarity of the Abolition Society is this: it is a voluntary association in one section of the country, designed to awaken public sentiment against a moral evil existing in another section of the country, and the principal point of effort seems to be, to enlarge the numbers of this association as a means of influencing public sentiment. The principal object of your proposed tour, I suppose, is to present facts, arguments, and persuasions to influence northern ladies to enrol themselves as members of this association.

I will therefore proceed to present some of the reasons which may be brought against such a measure as the one you would urge.

In the first place, the main principle of action in that society rests wholly on a false deduction from past experience. Experience has shown, that when certain moral evils exist in a community, efforts to awaken public sentiment against such practices, and combinations for the exercise of personal influence and example, have in various cases tended to rectify these evils. Thus in respect to intemperance;--the collecting of facts, the labours of public lecturers and the distribution of publications, have had much effect in diminishing the evil. So in reference to the slave-trade and slavery in England. The English nation possessed the power of regulating their own trade, and of giving liberty to every slave in their dominions; and yet they were entirely unmindful of their duty on this subject. Clarkson, Wilberforce, and their coadjutors, commenced a system of operations to arouse and influence public sentiment, and they succeeded in securing the suppression of the slave trade, and the gradual abolition of slavery in the English colonies. In both these cases, the effort was to enlighten and direct public sentiment in a community, of which the actors were a portion, in order to lead them to rectify an evil existing among THEMSELVES, which was entirely under their control.

From the success of such efforts, the Abolitionists of this country have drawn inferences, which appear to be not only illogical, but false. Because individuals in *their own* community have aroused their fellow citizens to correct their own evils, therefore they infer that attempts to convince their fellow-citizens of the faults of *another* community will lead that community to forsake their evil practices. An example will more clearly illustrate the case. Suppose two rival cities, which have always been in competition, and always jealous of each other's reputation and prosperity. Certain individuals in one of these cities become convinced, that the sin of intemperance is destroying their prosperity and domestic happiness. They proceed to collect facts, they arrange statistics, they call public meetings, they form voluntary associations, they use arguments, entreaties and personal example, and by these means they arrest the evil.

Suppose another set of men, in this same community, become convinced that certain practices in trade and business in the rival city, are dishonest, and have an oppressive bearing on certain classes in that city, and are injurious to the interests of general commerce. Suppose also, that these are practices, which, by those who allow them, are considered as honourable and right. Those who are convinced of their immorality, wish to alter the opinions and the practices of the citizens of their rival city, and to do this, they commence the collection of facts, that exhibit the tendencies of these practices and the evils they have engendered. But instead of going among the community in which the evils exist, and endeavouring to convince and persuade them, they proceed to form voluntary associations among their neighbours at home, and spend their time, money and efforts to convince their fellow citizens that the inhabitants of their rival city are guilty of a great sin. They also publish papers and tracts and send out agents, not to the guilty city, but to all the neighbouring towns and villages, to convince them of the sins of the city in their vicinity. And they claim that they shall succeed in making that city break off its sins, by these measures, because other men succeeded in banishing intemperance by labouring among their own friends and fellow citizens. Is not this example exactly parallel with the exertions of the Abolitionists? Are not the northern and southern sections of our country distinct communities, with different feelings and interests? Are they not rival, and jealous in feeling? Have the northern States the power to rectify evils at the South, as they have to remove their own moral deformities; or have they any such power over the southern States as the British people had over their own trade and their dependent colonies in the West Indies? Have not Abolitionists been sending out papers, tracts, and agents to convince the people of the North of the sins of the South? Have they not refrained from going to the South with their facts, arguments, and appeals, because they feared personal evils to themselves? And do not Abolitionists found their hopes of success in their project, on the success which crowned the efforts of British philanthropists in the case of slavery, and on the success that has attended efforts to banish intemperance? And do not these two cases differ entirely from the Abolition movement in this main point, that one is an effort to convince men of ***their own*** sins, and the other is an effort to convince men of the sins of ***other persons***?

The second reason I would urge against joining the Abolition Society is, that its character and measures are not either peaceful or Christian in tendency, but they rather are those which tend to generate party spirit, denunciation, recrimination, and angry passions.

But before bringing evidence to sustain this position, I wish to make a distinction between the ***men*** who constitute an association, and the ***measures*** which are advocated and adopted.

I believe, that as a body, Abolitionists are men of pure morals, of great honesty of purpose, of real benevolence and piety, and of great activity in efforts to promote what they consider the best interests of their fellow men. I believe, that, in making efforts to abolish slavery, they have taken measures, which they supposed were best calculated to bring this evil to an end, with the greatest speed, and with the least danger and suffering to the South. I do not believe they ever designed to promote disunion, or insurrection, or to stir up strife, or that they suppose that their measures can be justly characterized by the peculiarities I have specified. I believe they have been urged forward by a strong feeling of patriotism, as well as of religious duty, and that they have made great sacrifices of feeling, character, time, and money to promote what they believed to be the cause of humanity and the service of God. I regard individuals among them, as having taken a bold and courageous stand, in maintaining the liberty of free discussion, the liberty of speech and of the press; though this however is somewhat abated by the needless provocations by which they caused those difficulties and hazards they so courageously sustained. In speaking thus of Abolitionists as a body, it is not assumed that there are not bad men found in this party as well as in every other; nor that among those who are good men, there are not those who may have allowed party spirit to take the place of Christian principle; men who have exhibited a mournful destitution of Christian charity; who have indulged in an overbearing, denouncing, and self-willed pertinacity as to measures. Yet with these reservations, I believe that the above is no more than a fair and just exhibition of that class of men who are embraced in the party of Abolitionists. And all this can be admitted, and yet the objection I am to urge against joining their ranks may stand in its full force.

To make the position clearer, an illustration may be allowed. Suppose a body of good men become convinced that the inspired direction, "them that sin, rebuke before all, that others may fear," imposes upon them the duty of openly rebuking every body whom they discover in the practice of any sin. Suppose these men are daily in the habit of going into the streets, and calling all by-standers around them, pointing out certain men, some as liars, some as dishonest, some as licentious, and then bringing proofs of their guilt and rebuking them before all; at the same time exhorting all around to point at them the finger of scorn.

They persevere in this course till the whole community is thrown into an uproar; and assaults, and even bloodshed ensue. They then call on all good citizens to protect their persons from abuse, and to maintain the liberty of speech and of free opinion.

Now the men may be as pure in morals, as conscientious and upright in intention, as any Abolitionist, and yet every one would say, that their measures were unwise and unchristian.

In like manner, although Abolitionists may be lauded for many virtues, still much evidence can be presented, that the character and measures of the Abolition Society are not either peaceful or christian in tendency, but that they are in their nature calculated to generate party spirit, denunciation, recrimination, and angry passions.

The first thing I would present to establish this, is the character of the leaders of this association. Every combined effort is necessarily directed by leaders; and the spirit of the leaders will inevitably be communicated to their coadjutors, and appear in the measures of the whole body.

In attempting to characterize these leaders, I would first present another leader of a similar enterprise, the beloved and venerated WILBERFORCE. It is thus that his prominent traits are delineated by an intimate friend.

"His extreme benevolence contributed largely to his success. I have heard him say, that it was one of his constant rules, and on the question of slavery especially, never to provoke an adversary--to allow him credit fully for sincerity and purity of motive--to abstain from all irritating expressions--to avoid even such political attacks as would indispose his opponents for his great cause. In fact, the benignity, the gentleness, the kind-heartedness of the man, disarmed the bitterest foes. Not only on this question did he restrain himself, but generally. Once he had been called during a whole debate 'the religious member,' in a kind of scorn. He remarked afterwards, that he was much inclined to have retorted, by calling his opponent the *irreligious* member, but that he refrained, as it would have been a returning of evil for evil. Next to his general consistency, and love of the Scriptures, the *humility* of his character always appeared remarkable. The modest, shrinking, simple Christian statesman and friend always appeared in him. And the nearer you approached him, the more his habit of mind obviously appeared to be modest and lowly. His ***charity in judging of others***, is a farther trait of his Christian character. Of his benevolence I need not speak, but his ***kind construction of doubtful actions***, his ***charitable language*** toward those with whom he most widely differed, his thorough forgetfulness of little affronts, were fruits of that general benevolence which continually appeared."

This was the leader, both in and out of Parliament, of that body of men who combined to bring to an end slavery and the slave trade, in the dominions of Great Britain. With him, as principal leaders, were associated CLARKSON, SHARPE, MACAULAY, and others of a similar spirit. These men were all of them characterized by that mild, benevolent, peaceful, gentlemanly and forbearing spirit, which has been described as so conspicuous in Wilberforce. And when their measures are examined, it will be found that they were eminently mild, peaceful, and forbearing. Though no effort that is to encounter the selfish interests of men, can escape without odium and opposition, from those who are thwarted, and from all whom they can influence, these men carefully took those measures that were calculated to bring about their end with the least opposition and evil possible. They avoided prejudices, strove to conciliate opposers, shunned every thing that would give needless offence and exasperation, began slowly and cautiously, with points which could be the most easily carried, and advanced toward others only as public sentiment became more and more enlightened. They did not beard the lion in full face, by coming out as the first thing with the maxim, that all slavery ought and must be abandoned immediately. They began with "inquiries as to the ***impolicy*** of the ***slave trade***," and it was years before they came to the point of the abolition of slavery. And they carried their measures through, without producing warring parties among ***good men***, who held common principles with themselves. As a general fact, the pious men of Great Britain acted harmoniously in this great effort.

Let us now look at the leaders of the Abolition movement in America. The man who first took the lead was William L. Garrison, who, though he professes a belief in the Christian religion, is an avowed opponent of most of its institutions. The character and spirit of this man have for years been exhibited in "the Liberator," of which he is the editor. That there is to be found in that paper, or in any thing else, any evidence of his possessing the peculiar traits of Wilberforce, not even his warmest admirers will maintain. How many of the opposite traits can be found, those can best judge who have read his paper. Gradually others joined themselves in the effort commenced by Garrison; but for a long time they consisted chiefly of men who would fall into one of these three classes; either good men who were so excited by a knowledge of the enormous evils of slavery, that ***any thing*** was considered better than entire inactivity, or else men accustomed to a contracted field of observation, and more qualified to judge of immediate results than of general tendencies, or else men of ardent and impulsive temperament, whose feelings are likely to take the lead, rather than their judgment.

There are no men who act more efficiently as the leaders of an enterprise than the editors of the periodicals that advocate and defend it. The editors of the Emancipator, the Friend of Man, the New York Evangelist, and the other abolition periodicals, may therefore be considered as among the chief leaders of the enterprise, and their papers are the mirror from which their spirit and character are reflected.

I wish the friends of these editors would cull from their papers all the indications they can find of the peculiarities that distinguished Wilberforce and his associates; all the evidence of "a modest and lowly spirit,"--all the exhibitions of "charity in judging of the motives of those who oppose their measures,"--all the "indications of benignity, gentleness, and kind-heartedness,"--all the "kind constructions of doubtful actions,"--all the "charitable language used toward those who differ in opinion or measures,"--all the "thorough forgetfulness of little affronts,"--all the cases where "opponents are allowed full credit for purity and sincerity of motive,"--all cases where they have been careful "never to provoke an adversary,"--all cases where they have "refrained from all irritating expressions,"--all cases where they have avoided every thing that would "indispose their opponents for their great cause," and then compare the result with what may be found of an opposite character, and I think it would not be unsafe to infer that an association whose measures, on an exciting subject, were guided by such men, would be more likely to be aggressive than peaceful. The position I would establish will appear more clearly, by examining in detail some of the prominent measures which have been adopted by this association.

One of the first measures of Abolitionists was an attack on a benevolent society, originated and sustained by some of the most pious and devoted men of the age. It was imagined by Abolitionists, that the influence and measures of the Colonization Society tended to retard the abolition of slavery, and to perpetuate injurious prejudices against the coloured race. The peaceful and christian method of meeting this difficulty would have been, to collect all the evidence of this supposed hurtful tendency, and privately, and in a respectful and conciliating way, to have presented it to the attention of the wise and benevolent men, who were most interested in sustaining this institution. If this measure did not avail to convince them, then it would have been safe and justifiable to present to the public a temperate statement of facts, and of the deductions based on them, drawn up in a respectful and candid manner, with every charitable allowance which truth could warrant. Instead of this, when the attempt was first made to turn public opinion against the Colonization Society, I met one of the most influential supporters of that institution, just after he had had an interview with a leading Abolitionist. This gentleman was most remarkable for his urbanity, meekness, and benevolence, and his remark to me in reference to this interview, shows what was its nature. "I love truth and sound argument," said he, "but when a man comes at me with a sledge hammer, I cannot help dodging." This is a specimen of their private manner of dealing. In public, the enterprise was attacked as a plan for promoting the selfish interests and prejudices of the whites, at the expense of the coloured population; and in many cases, it was assumed that the conductors of this association were aware of this, and accessory to it. And the style in which the thing was done was at once offensive, inflammatory, and exasperating. Denunciation, sneers, and public rebuke, were bestowed indiscriminately upon the conductors of the enterprise, and of course they fell upon many sincere, upright, and conscientious men, whose feelings were harrowed by a sense of the injustice, the indecorum, and the unchristian treatment, they received. And when a temporary impression was made on the public mind, and its opponents supposed they had succeeded in crushing this society, the most public and triumphant exultation was not repressed. Compare this method of carrying a point, with that adopted by Wilberforce and his compeers, and I think you will allow that there was a way that was peaceful and christian, and that this was not the way which was chosen.

  The next measure of Abolitionism was an attempt to remove the prejudices of the whites against the blacks, on account of natural peculiarities. Now, prejudice is an ***unreasonable*** and ***groundless*** dislike of persons or things. Of course, as it is unreasonable, it is the most difficult of all things to conquer, and the worst and most irritating method that could be attempted would be, to attack a man as guilty of sin, as unreasonable, as ungenerous, or as proud, for allowing a certain prejudice.

This is the sure way to produce anger, self-justification, and an increase of the strength of prejudice, against that which has caused him this rebuke and irritation.

The best way to make a person like a thing which is disagreeable, is to try in some way to make it agreeable; and if a certain class of persons is the subject of unreasonable prejudice, the peaceful and christian way of removing it would be to endeavour to render the unfortunate persons who compose this class, so useful, so humble and unassuming, so kind in their feelings, and so full of love and good works, that prejudice would be supplanted by complacency in their goodness, and pity and sympathy for their disabilities. If the friends of the blacks had quietly set themselves to work to increase their intelligence, their usefulness, their respectability, their meekness, gentleness, and benevolence, and then had appealed to the pity, generosity, and christian feelings of their fellow citizens, a very different result would have appeared. Instead of this, reproaches, rebukes, and sneers, were employed to convince the whites that their prejudices were sinful, and without any just cause. They were accused of pride, of selfish indifference, of unchristian neglect. This tended to irritate the whites, and to increase their prejudice against the blacks, who thus were made the causes of rebuke and exasperation. Then, on the other hand, the blacks extensively received the Liberator, and learned to imbibe the spirit of its conductor.

They were taught to feel that they were injured and abused, the objects of a guilty and unreasonable prejudice--that they occupied a lower place in society than was right--that they ought to be treated as if they were whites; and in repeated instances, attempts were made by their friends to mingle them with whites, so as to break down the existing distinctions of society. Now, the question is not, whether these things, that were urged by Abolitionists, were true. The thing maintained is, that the method taken by them to remove this prejudice was neither peaceful nor christian in its tendency, but, on the contrary, was calculated to increase the evil, and to generate anger, pride, and recrimination, on one side, and envy, discontent, and revengeful feelings, on the other.

These are some of the general measures which have been exhibited in the Abolition movement. The same peculiarities may be as distinctly seen in specific cases, where the peaceful and quiet way of accomplishing the good was neglected, and the one most calculated to excite wrath and strife was chosen. Take, for example, the effort to establish a college for coloured persons. The quiet, peaceful, and christian way of doing such a thing, would have been, for those who were interested in the plan, to furnish the money necessary, and then to have selected a retired place, where there would be the least prejudice and opposition to be met, and there, in an unostentatious way, commenced the education of the youth to be thus sustained. Instead of this, at a time when the public mind was excited on the subject, it was noised abroad that a college for blacks was to be founded. Then a city was selected for its location, where was another college, so large as to demand constant effort and vigilance to preserve quiet subordination; where contests with "sailors and town boys" were barely kept at bay; a college embracing a large proportion of southern students, who were highly excited on the subject of slavery and emancipation; a college where half the shoe-blacks and waiters were coloured men. Beside the very walls of this college, it was proposed to found a college for coloured young men. Could it be otherwise than that opposition, and that for the best of reasons, would arise against such an attempt, both from the faculty of the college and the citizens of the place? Could it be reasonably expected that they would not oppose a measure so calculated to increase their own difficulties and liabilities, and at the same time so certain to place the proposed institution in the most unfavourable of all circumstances? But when the measure was opposed, instead of yielding meekly and peaceably to such reasonable objections, and soothing the feelings and apprehensions that had been excited, by putting the best construction on the matter, and seeking another place, it was claimed as an evidence of opposition to the interests of the blacks, and as a mark of the force of sinful prejudice. The worst, rather than the best, motives were ascribed to some of the most respectable, and venerated, and pious men, who opposed the measure; and a great deal was said and done that was calculated to throw the community into an angry ferment.

Take another example. If a prudent and benevolent female had selected almost any village in New England, and commenced a school for coloured females, in a quiet, appropriate, and unostentatious way, the world would never have heard of the case, except to applaud her benevolence, and the kindness of the villagers, who

## An Essay on Slavery and Abolitionism

aided her in the effort. But instead of this, there appeared public advertisements, (which I saw at the time,) stating that a seminary for the education of young ladies of colour was to be opened in Canterbury, in the state of Connecticut, where would be taught music on the piano forte, drawing, &c., together with a course of English education. Now, there are not a dozen coloured families in New England, in such pecuniary circumstances, that if they were whites it would not be thought ridiculous to attempt to give their daughters such a course of education, and Canterbury was a place where but few of the wealthiest families ever thought of furnishing such accomplishments for their children. Several other particulars might be added that were exceedingly irritating, but this may serve as a specimen of the method in which the whole affair was conducted. It was an entire disregard of the prejudices and the proprieties of society, and calculated to stimulate pride, anger, ill-will, contention, and all the bitter feelings that spring from such collisions. Then, instead of adopting measures to soothe and conciliate, rebukes, sneers and denunciations, were employed, and Canterbury and Connecticut were held up to public scorn and rebuke for doing what most other communities would probably have done, if similarly tempted and provoked.

Take another case. It was deemed expedient by Abolitionists to establish an Abolition paper, first in Kentucky, a slave State. It was driven from that State, either by violence or by threats. It retreated to Ohio, one of the free States. In selecting a place for its location, it might have been established in a small place, where the people were of similar views, or were not exposed to dangerous popular excitements. But Cincinnati was selected; and when the most intelligent, the most reasonable, and the most patriotic of the citizens remonstrated,--when they represented that there were peculiar and unusual liabilities to popular excitement on this subject,--that the organization and power of the police made it extremely dangerous to excite a mob, and almost impossible to control it,--that all the good aimed at could be accomplished by locating the press in another place, where there were not such dangerous liabilities,--when they kindly and respectfully urged these considerations, they were disregarded. I myself was present when a sincere friend urged upon the one who controlled that paper, the obligations of good men, not merely to avoid breaking wholesome laws themselves, but the duty of regarding the liabilities of others to temptation; and that where Christians could foresee that by placing certain temptations in the way of their fellow-men, all the probabilities were, that they would yield, and yet persisted in doing it, the tempters became partakers in the guilt of those who yielded to the temptation. But these remonstrances were ineffectual. The paper must not only be printed and circulated, but it must be stationed where were the greatest probabilities that measures of illegal violence would ensue. And when the evil was perpetrated, and a mob destroyed the press, then those who had urged on these measures of temptation, turned upon those who had advised and remonstrated, as the guilty authors of the violence, because, in a season of excitement, the measures adopted to restrain and control the mob, were not such as were deemed suitable and right.

Now, in all the above cases, I would by no means justify the wrong or the injudicious measures that may have been pursued, under this course of provocation. The greatness of temptation does by no means release men from obligation; but Christians are bound to remember that it is a certain consequence of throwing men into strong excitement, that they will act unwisely and wrong, and that the tempter as well as the tempted are held responsible, both by God and man. In all these cases, it cannot but appear that the good aimed at might have been accomplished in a quiet, peaceable, and christian way, and that this was not the way which was chosen.

The whole system of Abolition measures seems to leave entirely out of view, the obligation of Christians to save their fellow men from all needless temptations. If the thing to be done is only lawful and right, it does not appear to have been a matter of effort to do it in such a way as would not provoke and irritate; but often, if the chief aim had been to do the good in the most injurious and offensive way, no more certain and appropriate methods could have been devised.

So much has this been the character of Abolition movements, that many have supposed it to be a deliberate and systematized plan of the leaders to do nothing but what was strictly a ***right*** guaranteed by law, and yet, in such a manner, as to provoke men to anger, so that unjust and illegal acts might ensue, knowing, that as a consequence, the opposers of Abolition would be thrown into the wrong, and sympathy be aroused for Abolitionists as injured and persecuted men. It is a fact, that Abolitionists have taken the course most calculated to awaken illegal acts of violence, and that when they have ensued, they have seemed to rejoice in them, as calculated to advance and strengthen their cause. The violence of mobs, the denunciations and unreasonable requirements of the South, the denial of the right of petition, the restrictions attempted to be laid upon freedom of speech, and freedom of the press, are generally spoken of with exultation by Abolitionists, as what are among the chief means of promoting their cause. It is not so much by exciting feelings of pity and humanity, and Christian love, towards the oppressed, as it is by awakening indignation at the treatment of Abolitionists themselves, that their cause has prospered. How many men have declared or implied, that in joining the ranks of Abolition, they were influenced, not by their arguments, or by the wisdom of their course, but because the violence of opposers had identified that cause with the question of freedom of speech, freedom of the press, and civil liberty.

But when I say that many have supposed that it was the deliberate intention of the Abolitionists to foment illegal acts and violence, I would by no means justify a supposition, which is contrary to the dictates of justice and charity. The leaders of the Abolition Society disclaim all such wishes or intentions; they only act apparently on the assumption that they are exercising just rights, which they are not bound to give up, because other men will act unreasonably and wickedly.

Another measure of Abolitionists, calculated to awaken evil feelings, has been the treatment of those who objected to their proceedings.

A large majority of the philanthropic and pious, who hold common views with the Abolitionists, as to the sin and evils of slavery, and the duty of using all appropriate means to bring it to an end, have opposed their measures, because they have believed them not calculated to promote, but rather to retard the end proposed to be accomplished by them. The peaceful and Christian method of encountering such opposition, would have been to allow the opponents full credit for purity and integrity of motive, to have avoided all harsh and censorious language, and to have employed facts, arguments and persuasions, in a kind and respectful way with the hope of modifying their views and allaying their fears. Instead of this, the wise and good who opposed Abolition measures, have been treated as though they were the friends and defenders of slavery, or as those who, from a guilty, timid, time-serving policy, refused to take the course which duty demanded. They have been addressed either as if it were necessary to convince them that slavery is wrong and ought to be abandoned, or else, as if they needed to be exhorted to give up their timidity and selfish interest, and to perform a manifest duty, which they were knowingly neglecting.

Now there is nothing more irritating, when a man is conscientious and acting according to his own views of right, than to be dealt with in this manner. The more men are treated as if they were honest and sincere--the more they are treated with respect, fairness, and benevolence, the more likely they are to be moved by evidence and arguments. On the contrary, harshness, uncharitableness, and rebuke, for opinions and conduct that are in agreement with a man's own views of duty and rectitude, tend to awaken evil feelings, and indispose the mind properly to regard evidence. Abolitionists have not only taken this course, but in many cases, have seemed to act on the principle, that the abolition of Slavery, in the particular mode in which they were aiming to accomplish it, was of such paramount importance, that every thing must be overthrown that stood in the way.

No matter what respect a man had gained for talents, virtue, and piety, if he stood in the way of Abolitionism, he must be attacked as to character and motives. No matter how important an institution might be, if its influence was against the measures of Abolitionism, it must be attacked openly, or sapped privately, till its influence was destroyed. By such measures, the most direct means have been taken to awaken anger at injury, and resentment at injustice, and to provoke retaliation on those who inflict the wrong. All the partialities of personal friendship; all the feelings of respect accorded to good and useful men; all the interests that cluster around public institutions, entrenched in the hearts of the multitudes who sustain them, were outraged by such a course.

Another measure of Abolitionists, which has greatly tended to promote wrath and strife, is their indiscreet and incorrect use of terms.

To make this apparent, it must be premised, that words have no inherent meaning, but always signify that which they are commonly **understood** to mean. The question never should be asked, what *ought* a word to mean? but simply, what is the meaning generally attached to this word by those who use it? Vocabularies and standard writers are the proper umpires to decide this question. Now if men take words and give them a new and peculiar use, and are consequently misunderstood, they are guilty of a species of deception, and are accountable for all the evils that may ensue as a consequence.

For example; if physicians should come out and declare, that it was their opinion that they ought to poison all their patients, and they had determined to do it, and then all the community should be thrown into terror and excitement, it would be no justification for them to say, that all they intended by that language was, that they should administer as medicines, articles which are usually called poisons.

Now Abolitionists are before the community, and declare that all slavery is sin, which ought to be immediately forsaken; and that it is their object and intention to promote the ***immediate emancipation*** of all the slaves in this nation.

Now what is it that makes a man cease to be a slave and become free? It is not kind treatment from a master; it is not paying wages to the slave; it is not the intention to bestow freedom at a future time; it is not treating a slave as if he were free; it is not feeling toward a slave as if he were free. No instance can be found of any dictionary, or any standard writer, nor any case in common discourse, where any of these significations are attached to the word as constituting its peculiar and appropriate meaning. It always signifies ***that legal*** act, which, by the laws of the land, changes a slave to a freeman.

What then is the ***proper*** meaning of the language used by Abolitionists, when they say that all slavery is a sin which ought to be immediately abandoned, and that it is their object to secure the immediate emancipation of all slaves?

The true and only proper meaning of such language is, that it is the duty of every slave-holder in this nation, to go immediately and make out the legal instruments, that, by the laws of the land, change all his slaves to freemen. If their maxim is true, no exception can be made for those who live in States where the act of emancipation, by a master, makes a slave the property of the State, to be sold for the benefit of the State; and no exception can be made for those, who, by the will of testators, and by the law of the land, have no power to perform the legal act, which alone can emancipate their slaves.

To meet this difficulty, Abolitionists affirm, that, in such cases, men are physically unable to emancipate their slaves, and of course are not bound to do it; and to save their great maxim, maintain that, in such cases, the slaves are not slaves, and the slave-holders are not slave-holders, although all their legal relations remain unchanged.

The meaning which the Abolitionist attaches to his language is this, that every man is bound to treat his slaves, as nearly as he can, like freemen; and to use all his influence to bring the system of slavery to an end as soon as possible. And they allow that when men do this they are free from guilt, in the matter of slavery, and undeserving of censure.

But men at the North, and men at the South, understand the language used in its true and proper sense; and Abolitionists have been using these terms in a new and peculiar sense, which is inevitably and universally misunderstood, and this is an occasion of much of the strife and alarm which has prevailed both at the South and at the North. There are none but these defenders of slavery who maintain that it is a relation justifiable by the laws of the Gospel, who differ from Abolitionists in regard to the real thing which is meant. The great mistake of Abolitionists is in using terms which inculcate the immediate annihilation of the relation, when they only intend to urge the Christian duty of treating slaves according to the gospel rules of justice and benevolence, and using all lawful and appropriate means for bringing a most pernicious system to a speedy end.

If Abolitionists will only cease to teach that ***all*** slave-holding is a sin which ought to be ***immediately abolished***; if they will cease to urge their plan as one of ***immediate emancipation***, and teach simply and exactly that which they do mean, much strife and misunderstanding will cease. But so long as they persevere in using these terms in a new and peculiar sense, which will always be misunderstood, they are guilty of a species of deception and accountable for the evils that follow.

One other instance of a similar misuse of terms may be mentioned. The word "man-stealer" has one peculiar signification, and it is no more synonymous with "slave-holder" than it is with "sheep-stealer." But Abolitionists show that a slave-holder, in fact, does very many of the evils that are perpetrated by a man-stealer, and that the crime is quite as evil in its nature, and very similar in character, and, therefore, he calls a slave-holder a man-stealer.

On this principle there is no abusive language that may not be employed to render any man odious--for every man commits sin of some kind, and every sin is like some other sin, in many respects, and in certain aggravated cases, may be bad, or even worse, than another sin with a much more odious name. It is easy to show that a man who neglects all religious duty is very much like an atheist, and if he has had great advantages, and the atheist very few, he may be much more guilty than an atheist. And so, half the respectable men in our religious communities, may be called atheists, with as much propriety as a slave-holder can be called a man-stealer. Abolitionists have proceeded on this principle, in their various publications, until the terms of odium that have been showered upon slave-holders, would form a large page in the vocabulary of Billingsgate. This method of dealing with those whom we wish to convince and persuade, is as contrary to the dictates of common sense, as it is to the rules of good breeding and the laws of the gospel.

The preceding particulars are selected, as the evidence to be presented, that the character and measures of the Abolition Society are neither peaceful nor Christian in their tendency; but that in their nature they are calculated to generate party-spirit, denunciation, recrimination, and angry passions. If such be the tendency of this institution, it follows, that it is wrong for a Christian, or any lover of peace, to be connected with it.

The assertion that Christianity itself has led to strife and contention, is not a safe method of evading this argument. Christianity is a system of ***persuasion***, tending, by kind and gentle influences, to make men ***willing*** to leave off their sins--and it comes, not to convince those who are not sinners, but to sinners themselves.

Abolitionism, on the contrary, is a system of ***coercion*** by public opinion; and in its present operation, its influence is not to convince the erring, but to convince those who are not guilty, of the sins of those who are.

Another prominent peculiarity of the Abolitionists, (which is an objection to joining this association,) is their advocacy of a principle, which is wrong and very pernicious in its tendency. I refer to their views in regard to what is called "the doctrine of expediency." Their difficulty on this subject seems to have arisen from want of a clear distinction between the duty of those who are guilty of sin, and the duty of those who are aiming to turn men from their sins. The principle is assumed, that because certain men ought to abandon every sin immediately, therefore, certain other men are bound *immediately* to try and make them do it. Now the question of expediency does not relate to what men are bound to do, who are in the practice of sin themselves--for the immediate relinquishment of sin is the duty of all; but it relates to the duty of those who are to make efforts to induce others to break off their wickedness.

Here, the wisdom and rectitude of a given course, depend entirely on the ***probabilities of success***. If a father has a son of a very peculiar temperament, and he knows by observation, that the use of the rod will make him more irritable and more liable to a certain fault, and that kind arguments, and tender measures will more probably accomplish the desired object, it is a rule of expediency to try the most probable course. If a companion sees a friend committing a sin, and has, from past experience, learned that remonstrances excite anger and obstinacy, while a look of silent sorrow and disapprobation tends far more to prevent the evil, expediency and duty demand silence rather than remonstrance.

There are cases also, where differences in age, and station, and character, forbid all interference to modify the conduct and character of others.

A nursery maid may see that a father misgoverns his children, and ill-treats his wife. But her station makes it inexpedient for her to turn reprover. It is a case where reproof would do no good, but only evil.

So in communities, the propriety and rectitude of measures can be decided, not by the rules of duty that should govern those who are to renounce sin, but by the probabilities of good or evil consequence.

The Abolitionists seem to lose sight of this distinction. They form voluntary associations in free States, to convince their fellow citizens of the sins of other men in other communities. They are blamed and opposed, because their measures are deemed inexpedient, and calculated to increase, rather than diminish the evils to be cured.

In return, they show that slavery is a sin which ought to be abandoned immediately, and seem to suppose that it follows as a correct inference, that they themselves ought to engage in a system of agitation against it, and that it is needless for them to inquire whether preaching the truth in the manner they propose, will increase or diminish the evil. They assume that whenever sin is committed, not only ought the sinner immediately to cease, but all his fellow-sinners are bound to take measures to make him cease, and to take measures, without any reference to the probabilities of success.

That this is a correct representation of the views of Abolitionists generally, is evident from their periodicals and conversation. All their remarks about preaching the truth and leaving consequences to God--all their depreciation of the doctrine of expediency, are rendered relevant only by this supposition.

The impression made by their writings is, that God has made rules of duty; that all men are in all cases to remonstrate against the violation of those rules; and that God will take the responsibility of bringing good out of this course; so that we ourselves are relieved from any necessity of inquiring as to probable results.

If this be not the theory of duty adopted by this association, then they stand on common ground with those who oppose their measures, viz: that the propriety and duty of a given course is to be decided by ***probabilities as to its results***; and these probabilities are to be determined by the ***known laws of mind***, and the ***records of past experience***.

For only one of two positions can be held. Either that it is the duty of all men to remonstrate at all times against all violations of duty, and leave the consequences with God; or else that men are to use their judgment, and take the part of remonstrance only at such a time and place, and in such a manner, as promise the best results.

That the Abolitionists have not held the second of these positions, must be obvious to all who have read their documents. It would therefore be unwise and wrong to join an association which sustains a principle false in itself, and one which, if acted out, would tend to wrath and strife and every evil word and work.

Another reason, and the most important of all, against promoting the plans of the Abolitionists, is involved in the main question--what are the probabilities as to the results of their movements? The only way to judge of the future results of certain measures is, by the known laws of mind, and the recorded experience of the past.

Now what is the evil to be cured?

# SLAVERY IN THIS NATION.

That this evil is at no distant period to come to an end, is the unanimous opinion of all who either notice the tendencies of the age, or believe in the prophecies of the Bible. All who act on Christian principles in regard to slavery, believe that in a given period (variously estimated) it will end. The only question then, in regard to the benefits to be gained, or the evils to be dreaded in the present agitation of the subject, relates to the ***time*** and the ***manner*** of its extinction. The Abolitionists claim that their method will bring it to an end in the shortest time, and in the safest and best way. Their opponents believe, that it will tend to bring it to an end, if at all, at the most distant period, and in the most dangerous way.

As neither party are gifted with prescience, and as the Deity has made no revelations as to the future results of any given measures, all the means of judging that remain to us, as before stated, are the laws of mind, and the records of the past.

The position then I would aim to establish is, that the method taken by the Abolitionists is the one that, according to the laws of mind and past experience, is least likely to bring about the results they aim to accomplish. The general statement is this.

The object to be accomplished is:

First. To convince a certain community, that they are in the practice of a great sin, and

Secondly. To make them willing to relinquish it.

The method taken to accomplish this is, by voluntary associations in a foreign community, seeking to excite public sentiment against the perpetrators of the evil; exhibiting the enormity of the crime in full measure, without palliation, excuse or sympathy, by means of periodicals and agents circulating, not in the community committing the sin, but in that which does not practise it.

Now that this method may, in conjunction with other causes, have an influence to bring slavery to an end, is not denied. But it is believed, and from the following considerations, that it is the least calculated to do the *good*, and that it involves the greatest evils.

It is a known law of mind first seen in the nursery and school, afterwards developed in society, that a person is least likely to judge correctly of truth, and least likely to yield to duty, when excited by passion.

It is a law of experience, that when wrong is done, if repentance and reformation are sought, then love and kindness, mingled with remonstrance, coming from one who has a *right* to speak, are more successful than rebuke and scorn from others who are not beloved, and who are regarded as impertinent intruders.

In the nursery, if the child does wrong, the finger of scorn, the taunting rebuke, or even the fair and deserved reproof of equals, will make the young culprit only frown with rage, and perhaps repeat and increase the injury. But the voice of maternal love, or even the gentle remonstrances of an elder sister, may bring tears of sorrow and contrition.

So in society. Let a man's enemies, or those who have no interest in his welfare, join to rebuke and rail at his offences, and no signs of penitence will be seen. But let the clergyman whom he respects and loves, or his bosom friend approach him, with kindness, forbearance and true sincerity, and all that is possible to human agency will be effected.

It is the maxim then of experience, that when men are to be turned from evils, and brought to repent and reform, those only should interfere who are most loved and respected, and who have the best right to approach the offender. While on the other hand, rebuke from those who are deemed obtrusive and inimical, or even indifferent, will do more harm than good.

It is another maxim of experience, that such dealings with the erring should be in private, not in public. The moment a man is publicly rebuked, shame, anger, and pride of opinion, all combine to make him defend his practice, and refuse either to own himself wrong, or to cease from his evil ways.

The Abolitionists have violated all these laws of mind and of experience, in dealing with their southern brethren.

Their course has been most calculated to awaken anger, fear, pride, hatred, and all the passions most likely to blind the mind to truth, and make it averse to duty.

They have not approached them with the spirit of love, courtesy, and forbearance.

They are not the persons who would be regarded by the South, as having any *right* to interfere; and therefore, whether they have such right or not, the probabilities of good are removed. For it is not only demanded for the benefit of the offender, that there should really be a right, but it is necessary that he should feel that there is such a right.

In dealing with their brethren, too, they have not tried silent, retired, private measures. It has been public denunciation of crime and shame in newspapers, addressed as it were to by-standers, in order to arouse the guilty.

In reply to this, it has been urged, that men could not go to the South--that they would be murdered there--that the only way was, to convince the North, and excite public odium against the sins of the South, and thus gradually conviction, repentance, and reformation would ensue.

Here is another case where men are to judge of their duty, by estimating probabilities of future results; and it may first be observed, that it involves the principle of expediency, in just that form to which Abolitionists object.

It is allowed that the immediate abolition of slavery is to be produced by means of "light and love," and yet it is maintained as right to withdraw personally from the field of operation, because of ***consequences***; because of the probable danger of approaching. "If we go to the South, and present truth, argument, and entreaty, ***we shall be slain***, and therefore we are not under obligation to go." If this justifies Abolitionists in their neglect of their offending brethren, because they fear evil results to themselves, it also justifies those who refuse to act with Abolitionists in their measures, because they fear other evil results.

But what proof is there, that if the Abolitionists had taken another method, the one more in accordance with the laws of mind and the dictates of experience, that there would have been at the South all this violence? Before the abolition movement commenced, both northern and southern men, expressed their views freely at the South. The dangers, evils, and mischiefs of slavery were exhibited and discussed even in the legislative halls of more than one of the Southern States, and many minds were anxiously devising measures, to bring this evil to an end.

Now let us look at some of the records of past experience. Clarkson was the first person who devoted himself to the cause of Abolition in England. His object was to convince the people of England that they were guilty of a great impolicy, and great sin, in permitting the slave-trade. He was to meet the force of public sentiment, and power, and selfishness, and wealth, which sustained this traffic, in that nation. What were his measures? He did not go to Sweden, or Russia, or France, to awaken public sentiment against the sins of the English.--He began by first publishing an inquiry in England whether it was right to seize men, and make them slaves. He went unostentatiously to some of the best and most pious men there, and endeavoured to interest them in the inquiry.

Then he published an article on the impolicy of the slave-trade, showing its disadvantages. Then he collected information of the evils and enormities involved in the traffic, and went quietly around among those most likely to be moved by motives of humanity and Christianity. In this manner he toiled for more than fourteen years, slowly implanting the leaven among the good men, until he gained a noble band of patriots and Christians, with Wilberforce at their head.

The following extract from a memoir of Clarkson discloses the manner and spirit in which he commenced his enterprise, and toiled through to its accomplishment.

"In 1785 Dr. Peckhard, Vice-Chancellor of the University, deeply impressed with the iniquity of the slave-trade, announced as a subject for a Latin Dissertation to the Senior Bachelors of Arts: 'Anne liceat invitos in servitutem dare?' 'Is it right to make slaves of others against their will?' However benevolent the feelings of the Vice-Chancellor, and however strong and clear the opinions he held on the inhuman traffic, it is probable that he little thought that this discussion would secure for the object so dear to his own heart, efforts and advocacy equally enlightened and efficient, that should be continued, until his country had declared, not that the slave-trade only, but that slavery itself should cease.

"Mr. Clarkson, having in the preceding year gained the first prize for the Latin Dissertation, was naturally anxious to maintain his honourable position; and no efforts were spared, during the few intervening weeks, in collecting information and evidence. Important facts were gained from Anthony Benezet's Historical Account of Guinea, which Mr. Clarkson hastened to London to purchase. Furnished with these and other valuable information, he commenced his difficult task. How it was accomplished, he thus informs us.

"'No person,' he states,[1] 'can tell the severe trial which the writing of it proved to me. I had expected pleasure from the invention of the arguments, from the arrangement of them, from the putting of them together, and from the thought, in the interim, that I was engaged in an innocent contest for literary honour. But all my pleasure was damped by the facts which were now continually before me. It was but one gloomy subject from morning to night. In the day-time I was uneasy; in the night I had little rest. I sometimes never closed my eyelids for grief. It became now not so much a trial for academical reputation, as for the production of a work which might be useful to injured Africa. And keeping this idea in my mind ever after the perusal of Benezet, I always slept with a candle in my room, that I might rise out of bed, and put down such thoughts as might occur to me in the night, if I

---

1 History of the Abolition of the Slave Trade.

judged them valuable, conceiving that no arguments of any moment should be lost in so great a cause. Having at length finished this painful task, I sent my Essay to the Vice-Chancellor, and soon afterwards found myself honoured, as before, with the first prize.

"'As it is usual to read these essays publicly in the senate-house soon after the prize is adjudged, I was called to Cambridge for this purpose. I went, and performed my office. On returning, however, to London, the subject of it almost wholly engrossed my thoughts. I became at times very seriously affected while upon the road. I stopped my horse occasionally, and dismounted, and walked. I frequently tried to persuade myself in these intervals that the contents of my Essay could not be true. The more, however, I reflected upon them, or rather upon the authorities on which they were founded, the more I gave them credit. Coming in sight of Wade's Mill, in Hertfordshire, I sat down disconsolate on the turf by the road-side, and held my horse. Here a thought came into my mind, that if the contents of the Essay were true, it was time some person should see these calamities to their end. Agitated in this manner, I reached home. This was in the summer of 1785.

"'In the course of the autumn of the same year I experienced similar impressions. I walked frequently into the woods, that I might think on the subject in solitude, and find relief to my mind there. But there the question still recurred, 'Are these things true?' Still the answer followed as instantaneously,--'They are.' Still the result accompanied it; 'Then, surely, some person should interfere.' I then began to envy those who had seats in parliament, and who had great riches, and widely extended connexions, which would enable them to take up this cause. Finding scarcely any one at that time who thought of it, I was turned frequently to myself. But here many difficulties arose. It struck me, among others, that a young man of only twenty-four years of age could not have that solid judgment, or knowledge of men, manners, and things, which were requisite to qualify him to undertake a task of such magnitude and importance: and with whom was I to unite? I believed also, that it looked so much like one of the feigned labours of Hercules, that my understanding would be suspected if I proposed it. On ruminating, however, on the subject, I found one thing at least practicable, and that this was also in my power. I could translate my Latin Dissertation. I could enlarge it usefully. I could see how the public received it, or how far they were likely to favour any serious measures, which should have a tendency to produce the abolition of the slave-trade. Upon this, then, I determined; and in the middle of the month of November, 1785, I began my work.'

"Such is the characteristic and ingenuous account given by Clarkson of his introduction to that work to which the energies of his life were devoted, and in reference to which, and to the account whence the foregoing extract has been made, one of the most benevolent and gifted writers of our country[2] has justly observed,--

"'This interesting tale is related, not by a descendant, but a cotemporary; not by a distant spectator, but by a participator of the contest; and of all the many participators, by the man confessedly the most efficient; the man whose unparalleled labours in this work of love and peril, leave on the mind of a reflecting reader the sublime doubt, which of the two will have been the greater final gain to the moral world,--the removal of the evil, or the proof, thereby given, what mighty effects single good men may realize by self-devotion and perseverance.'

"When Mr. Clarkson went to London to publish his book, he was introduced to many friends of the cause of Abolition, who aided in giving it extensive circulation. Whilst thus employed, he received an invitation, which he accepted, to visit the Rev. James Ramsay, vicar of Teston, in Kent, who had resided nineteen years in the island of St. Christopher.

"Shortly afterwards, dining one day at Sir Charles Middleton's, (afterwards Lord Barham,) the conversation turned upon the subject, and Mr. Clarkson declared that he was ready to devote himself to the cause. This avowal met with great encouragement from the company, and Sir C. Middleton, then Comptroller to the Navy, offered every possible assistance. The friends of Mr. Clarkson increased, and this encouraged him to proceed. Dr. Porteus, then Bishop of Chester, and Lord Scarsdale, were secured in the House of Lords. Mr. Bennet Langton, and Dr. Baker, who were acquainted with many members of both houses of parliament; the honoured Granville Sharpe, James and Richard Phillips, could be depended upon, as well as the entire body of the Society of Friends, to many of whom he had been introduced by Mr. Joseph Hancock, his fellow-townsman. Seeking information in every direction, Mr. Clarkson boarded a number of vessels engaged in the African trade, and obtained specimens of the natural productions of the country. The beauty of the

---

2   Coleridge.

cloth made from African cotton, &c. enhanced his estimate of the skill and ingenuity of the people, and gave a fresh stimulus to his exertions on their behalf. He next visited a slave-ship; the rooms below, the gratings above, and the barricade across the deck, with the explanation of their uses, though the sight of them filled him with sadness and horror, gave new energy to all his movements. In his indefatigable endeavours to collect evidence and facts, he visited most of the sea-ports in the kingdom, pursuing his great object with invincible ardour, although sometimes at the peril of his life. The following circumstance, among others, evinces the eminent degree in which he possessed that untiring perseverance, on which the success of a great enterprise often depends.

"Clarkson and his friends had reason to fear that slaves brought from the interior of Africa by certain rivers, had been kidnapped; and it was deemed of great importance to ascertain the fact. A friend one day mentioned to Mr. Clarkson, that he had, above twelve months before, seen a sailor who had been up these rivers. The name of the sailor was unknown, and all the friend could say was, that he was going to, or belonged to, some man-of-war in ordinary. The evidence of this individual was important, and, aided by his friend Sir Charles Middleton, who gave him permission to board all the ships of war in ordinary, Mr. Clarkson commenced his search:--beginning at Deptford, he visited successfully Woolwich, Chatham, Sheerness, and Portsmouth; examining in his progress the different persons on board upwards of two hundred and sixty vessels, without discovering the object of his search. The feelings under which the search was continued, and the success with which it was crowned, he has himself thus described:--

"'Matters now began to look rather disheartening,--I mean as far as my grand object was concerned. There was but one other port left, and this was between two and three hundred miles distant. I determined, however, to go to Plymouth. I had already been more successful in this tour, with respect to obtaining general evidence, than in any other of the same length; and the probability was, that as I should continue to move among the same kind of people, my success would be in a similar proportion, according to the number visited. These were great encouragements to me to proceed. At length I arrived at the place of my last hope. On my first day's expedition I boarded forty vessels, but found no one in these who had been on the coast of Africa in the slave-trade. One or two had been there in king's ships; but they never had been on shore. Things were now drawing near to a close; and notwithstanding my success, as to general evidence, in this journey, my heart began to beat. I was restless and uneasy during the night. The next morning I felt agitated again between the alternate pressure of hope and fear; and in this state I entered my boat. The fifty-seventh vessel I boarded was the Melampus frigate.-- One person belonging to it, on examining him in the captain's cabin, said he had been two voyages to Africa; and I had not long discoursed with him, before I found, to my inexpressible joy, that he was the man. I found, too, that he unravelled the question in dispute precisely as our inferences had determined it. He had been two expeditions up the river Calabar, in the canoes of the natives. In the first of these they came within a certain distance of a village: they then concealed themselves under the bushes, which hung over the water from the banks. In this position they remained during the day-light; but at night they went up to it armed, and seized all the inhabitants who had not time to make their escape. They obtained forty-five persons in this manner. In the second, they were out eight or nine days, when they made a similar attempt, and with nearly similar success. They seized men, women, and children, as they could find them in the huts. They then bound their arms, and drove them before them to the canoes. The name of the person thus discovered on board of the Melampus was Isaac Parker. On inquiring into his character, from the master of the division, I found it highly respectable. I found also afterward that he had sailed with Captain Cook, with great credit to himself, round the world. It was also remarkable, that my brother, on seeing him in London, when he went to deliver his evidence, recognized him as having served on board the Monarch, man-of-war, and as one of the most exemplary men in that ship.'

"Mr. Clarkson became, early in his career, acquainted with Mr. Wilberforce. At their first interview, the latter frankly stated, 'that the subject had often employed his thoughts, and was near his heart,' and learning his visitor's intention to devote himself to this benevolent object, congratulated him on his decision; desired to be made acquainted with his progress, expressing his willingness, in return, to afford every assistance in his power. In his intercourse with members of parliament, Mr. Clarkson was now frequently associated with Mr. Wilberforce, who daily became more interested in the fate of Africa. The intercourse of the two philanthropists was mutually cordial and encouraging; Mr. Clarkson imparting his discoveries in the custom-houses of London, Liverpool, and other places; and Mr. Wilberforce communicating the information he had gained from those with whom he associated.

"In 1788, Mr. Clarkson published his important work on the Impolicy of the Slave-Trade.

"In 1789, this indefatigable man went to France, by the advice of the Committee which he had been instrumental in forming two years before; Mr. Wilberforce, always solicitous for the good of the oppressed Africans, being of opinion that advantage might be taken of the commotions in that country, to induce the leading persons there to take the slave-trade into their consideration, and incorporate it among the abuses to be removed. Several of Mr. Clarkson's friends advised him to travel by another name, as accounts had arrived in England of the excesses which had taken place in Paris; but to this he could not consent. On his arrival in that city he was speedily introduced to those who were favourable to the great object of his life; and at the house of M. Necker dined with the six deputies of colour from St. Domingo,--who had been sent to France at this juncture, to demand that the free people of colour in their country might be placed upon an equality with the whites. Their communications to the English philanthropist were important and interesting; they hailed him as their friend, and were abundant in their commendations of his conduct.

"Copies of the Essay on the Impolicy of the Slave-Trade, translated into French, with engravings of the plan and section of a slave ship, were distributed with apparent good effect. The virtuous Abbe Gregoire, and several members of the National Assembly, called upon Mr. Clarkson. The Archbishop of Aix was so struck with horror, when the plan of the slave ship was shown to him, that he could scarcely speak; and Mirabeau ordered a model of it in wood to be placed in his dining-room.

"The circulation of intelligence, although contributing to make many friends, called forth the extraordinary exertions of enemies. Merchants, and others interested in the continuance of the slave-trade, wrote letters to the Archbishop of Aix, beseeching him not to ruin France; which they said he would inevitably do, if, as the president, he were to grant a day for hearing the question of the abolition. Offers of money were made to Mirabeau, if he would totally abandon his intended motion. Books were circulated in opposition to Mr. Clarkson's; resort was had to the public papers, and he was denounced as a spy. The clamour raised by these efforts pervaded all Paris, and reached the ears of the king. M. Necker had a long conversation with his royal master upon it, who requested to see the Essay, and the specimens of African manufactures, and bestowed considerable time upon them, being surprised at the state of the arts there. M. Necker did not exhibit the section of the slave ship, thinking that as the king was indisposed, he might be too much affected by it. Louis returned the specimens, commissioning M. Necker to convey his thanks to Mr. Clarkson, and express his gratification at what he had seen.

"No decided benefit appears at this time to have followed the visit: but though much depressed by his ill success in France, Mr. Clarkson continued his labours, till excess of exertion, joined to repeated and bitter disappointments, impaired his health, and, after a hard struggle, subdued a constitution, naturally strong and vigorous beyond the lot of men in general, but shattered by anxiety and fatigue, and the sad probability, often forced upon his understanding, that all might at last have been in vain. Under these feelings, he retired in 1794 to the beautiful banks of Ulleswater; there to seek that rest which, without peril to his life, could no longer be delayed.

"For seven years he had maintained a correspondence with four hundred persons; he annually wrote a book upon the subject of the abolition, and travelled more than thirty-five thousand miles in search of evidence, making a great part of these journeys in the night. 'All this time,' Mr. Clarkson writes, 'my mind had been on the stretch; it had been bent too to this one subject; for I had not even leisure to attend to my own concerns. The various instances of barbarity, which had come successively to my knowledge within this period, had vexed, harassed, and afflicted it. The wound which these had produced was rendered still deeper by the reiterated refusal of persons to give their testimony, after I had travelled hundreds of miles in quest of them. But the severest stroke was that inflicted by the persecution begun and pursued by persons interested in the continuance of the trade, of such witnesses as had been examined against them; and whom, on account of their dependent situation in life, it was most easy to oppress. As I had been the means of bringing them forward on these occasions, they naturally came to me, as the author of their miseries and their ruin.³ These different circumstances, by acting together, had at length brought me into the situation just mentioned; and I was, therefore, obliged, though very reluctantly, to be borne out of the field where I had placed the great honour and glory of my life.'"

It was while thus recruiting the energies exhausted in the conflict, that Clarkson, and the compatriot band with which he had been associated in the long and arduous struggle, were crowned with victory, and received the grateful reward of their honourable toil in the final abolition of the slave-trade by the British nation, in 1807, the last but most glorious act of the Grenville administration.

The preceding shows something of the career of Clarkson while labouring to convince the people of Great Britain of the iniquity of ***their own*** trade, a trade which they had the power to abolish. During all this time, Clarkson, Wilberforce, and their associates avoided touching the matter of *slavery*. They knew that one thing must be gained at a time, and they as a matter of expediency, avoided discussing the duty of the British nation in regard to the system of slavery in their Colonies which was entirely under their own control. During all the time that was employed in efforts to end the slave-trade, slavery was existing in the control of the British people, and yet Clarkson and Wilberforce decided that it was right to let that matter entirely alone.

The following shows Clarkson's proceedings after the British nation had abolished the slave-trade.

"By the publication of his Thoughts on the Abolition of Slavery, Mr. Clarkson showed that neither he nor those connected with him, considered their work as accomplished, when the laws of his country clasped with its felons those engaged in the nefarious traffic of slaves. But the efforts of Mr. Clarkson were not confined to his pen. In 1818, he proceeded to Aix la Chapelle, at the time when the sovereigns of Europe met in congress. He was received with marked attention by the Emperor of Russia, who listened to his statements (respecting the *slave-trade*,) and promised to use his influence with the assembled monarchs, to secure the entire suppression of the trade in human beings, as speedily as possible. Describing his interview

---

3 The father of the late Samuel Whitbread, Esq., generously undertook, in order to make Mr. Clarkson's mind easy upon the subject, "to make good all injuries which any individuals might suffer from such persecution;" and he honourably and noblyfulfilled his engagement.

with this amiable monarch, in which the subject of peace societies, as well as the abolition of the slave-trade was discussed, Mr. Clarkson, in a letter to a friend, thus writes:

"'It was about nine at night, when I was shown into the emperor's apartment. I found him alone. He met me at the door, and shaking me by the hand, said, 'I had the pleasure of making your acquaintance at Paris.' He then led me some little way into the room, and leaving me there, went forward and brought me a chair with his own hand, and desired me to sit down. This being done, he went for another chair, and bringing it very near to mine, placed himself close to me, so that we sat opposite to each other.

"'I began the conversation by informing the emperor that as I supposed the congress of Aix la Chapelle might possibly be the last congress of sovereigns for settling the affairs of Europe, its connexions and dependencies, I had availed myself of the kind permission he gave me at Paris, of applying to him in behalf of the oppressed Africans, being unwilling to lose the last opportunity of rendering him serviceable to the cause.

"'The emperor replied, that he had read both my letter and my address to the sovereigns, and that what I asked him and the other sovereigns to do, was only reasonable.

"'Here I repeated the two great propositions in the address--the necessity of bringing the Portuguese time for continuing the trade (which did not expire till 1825, and then only with a condition,) down to the Spanish time, which expired in 1820; and secondly, when the two times should legally have expired, (that is, both of them in 1820,) then to make any farther continuance *piracy*. I entreated him not to be deceived by any other propositions; for that Mr. Wilberforce, myself, and others, who had devoted our time to this subject, were sure that no other measure would be effectual.

"'He then said very feelingly in these words, 'By the providence of God, I and my kingdom have been saved from a merciless tyranny, (alluding to the invasion of Napoleon,) and I should but ill repay the blessing, if I were not to do every thing in my power to protect the poor Africans against their oppression also.'

"'The emperor then asked if he could do any thing else for our cause. I told him he could; and that I should be greatly obliged to him if he would present one of the addresses to the Emperor of Austria, and another to the King of Prussia, ***with his own hand***. I had brought two of them in my pocket for the purpose. He asked me why I had not presented them before. I replied that I had not the honour of knowing either of those sovereigns as I knew him; nor any of their ministers; and that I was not only fearful lest these addresses would not be presented to them, but even if they were, that coming into their hands without any recommendation, they would be laid aside and not read; on the other hand, if he (the emperor,) would condescend to present them, I was sure they would be read, and that coming from him, they would come with a weight of influence, which would secure an attention to their contents. Upon this, the emperor promised, in the most kind and affable manner, that he would perform the task I had assigned to him.

"'We then rose from our seats to inspect some articles of manufacture, which I had brought with me as a present to him, and which had been laid upon the table. We examined the articles in leather first, one by one, with which he was uncommonly gratified. He said they exhibited not only genius but taste. He inquired if they tanned their own leather, and how: I replied to his question. He said he had never seen neater work, either in Petersburg or in London. He then looked at a dagger and its scabbard or sheath. I said the sheath was intended as a further, but more beautiful specimen of the work of the poor Africans in leather; and the blade of their dagger as a specimen of their work in iron. Their works in cotton next came under our notice. There was one piece which attracted his particular notice, and which was undoubtedly very beautiful. It called from him this observation, 'Manchester,' said he, 'I think is your great place for manufactures of this sort--do you think they could make a better piece of cotton there?' I told him I had never seen a better piece of workmanship of the kind any where. Having gone over all the articles, the emperor desired me to inform him whether he was to understand that these articles were made by the Africans in their own country, that is, in their native villages, or ***after they had arrived in America***, where they would have an opportunity of seeing European manufactures, and experienced workmen in the arts? I replied that such articles might be found in every African village, both on the coast and in the interior, and that they were samples of their own ingenuity, without any connexion with Europeans. 'Then,' said the emperor, 'you astonish me-- you have given me a new idea of the state of these poor people. I was not aware that they were so advanced in society. The works you have shown me are not the works of brutes--but of men, endued with rational and intellectual powers, and capable of being brought to as high a degree of proficiency as any other men. ***Africa ought to have a fair chance of raising her character in the scale of the civilized world.*** ' I replied that it was this cruel traffic alone, which had prevented Africa from rising to a level with other nations; and that it was only astonishing to me that the natives there had, under its impeding influence, arrived at the perfection which had displayed itself in the specimens of workmanship he had just seen.'"

Animated by a growing conviction of the righteousness of the cause in which he was engaged, and encouraged by the success with which past endeavours had been crowned, Mr. Clarkson continued his efficient co-operation with the friends of Abolition, advocating its claims on all suitable occasions.

It would be superfluous to recount the steps by which, even before the venerated Wilberforce was called to his rest, this glorious event was realized, and Clarkson beheld the great object of his own life, and those with whom he had acted, triumphantly achieved. The gratitude cherished towards the Supreme Ruler for the boon thus secured to the oppressed--the satisfaction which a review of past exertions afforded, were heightened by the joyous sympathy of a large portion of his countrymen.[4]

The History of the Abolition of the Slave-trade, by Clarkson himself, presents a more detailed account of his own labours and of the labours of others, and whoever will read it, will observe the following particulars in which this effort differed from the Abolition movement in America.

In the first place, it was conducted by some of the wisest and most talented statesmen, as well as the most pious men, in the British nation. Pitt, Fox, and some of the highest of the nobility and bishops in England, were the firmest friends of the enterprise from the first. It was conducted by men who had the intellect, knowledge, discretion, and wisdom demanded for so great an enterprise.

Secondly. It was conducted slowly, peaceably, and by eminently judicious influences.

Thirdly. It included, to the full extent, the doctrine of expediency denounced

---

4  This account of Clarkson, and the preceding one of Wilberforce, are taken from the Christian Keepsake of 1836 and 1837.

by Abolitionists.

One of the first decisions of the "Committee for the Abolition of the Slave-trade," which conducted all Abolition movements, was that *slavery* should not be attacked, but only the *slave-trade*; and Clarkson expressly says, that it was owing to this, more than to any other measure, that success was gained.

Fourthly. Good men were not divided, and thrown into contending parties.--The opponents to the measure, were only those who were personally interested in the perpetuation of slavery or the slave-trade.

Fifthly. This effort was one to convince men of their *own* obligations, and not an effort to arouse public sentiment against the sinful practices of another community over which they had no control.

I would now ask, why could not some southern gentleman, such for example as Mr. Birney, whose manners, education, character, and habits give him abundant facilities, have acted the part of Clarkson, and quietly have gone to work at the South, collecting facts, exhibiting the impolicy and the evils, to good men at the South, by the fire-side of the planter, the known home of hospitality and chivalry. Why could he not have commenced with the most vulnerable point, the ***domestic slave-trade***, leaving emancipation for a future and more favourable period? What right has any one to say that there was no southern Wilberforce that would have arisen, no southern Grant, Macaulay or Sharpe, who, like the English philanthropists, would have stood the fierce beating of angry billows, and by patience, kindness, arguments, facts, eloquence, and Christian love, convinced the skeptical, enlightened the ignorant, excited the benevolent, and finally have carried the day at the South, by the same means and measures, as secured the event in England? All experience is in favour of the method which the Abolitionists have rejected, because it involves ***danger to themselves***. The cause they have selected is one that stands alone.--No case parallel on earth can be brought to sustain it, with probabilities of good results. No instance can be found, where exciting the public sentiment of one community against evil practices in another, was ever made the means of eradicating those evils. All the laws of mind, all the records of experience, go against the measures that Abolitionists have taken, and in favour of the one they have rejected. And when we look still farther ahead, at results which time is to develope, how stand the probabilities, when we, in judging, again take, as data, the laws of mind

# An Essay on Slavery and Abolitionism

and the records of experience?

What are the plans, hopes, and expectations of Abolitionists, in reference to their measures? They are now labouring to make the North a great Abolition Society,--to convince every northern man that slavery at the South is a great sin, and that it ought immediately to cease. Suppose they accomplish this to the extent they hope,--so far as we have seen, the more the North is convinced, the more firmly the South rejects the light, and turns from the truth.

While Abolition Societies did not exist, men could talk and write, at the South, against the evils of slavery, and northern men had free access and liberty of speech, both at the South and at the North. But now all is changed. Every avenue of approach to the South is shut. No paper, pamphlet, or preacher, that touches on that topic, is admitted in their bounds. Their own citizens, that once laboured and remonstrated, are silenced; their own clergy, under the influence of the exasperated feelings of their people, and their own sympathy and sense of wrong, either entirely hold their peace, or become the defenders of a system they once lamented, and attempted to bring to an end. This is the record of experience as to the tendencies of Abolitionism, as thus far developed. The South are now in just that state of high exasperation, at the sense of wanton injury and impertinent interference, which makes the influence of truth and reason most useless and powerless.

But suppose the Abolitionists succeed, not only in making northern men Abolitionists, but also in sending a portion of light into the South, such as to form a body of Abolitionists there also. What is the thing that is to be done to end slavery at the South? It is to ***alter the laws***, and to do this, a small minority must begin a long, bitter, terrible conflict with a powerful and exasperated majority. Now if, as the Abolitionists hope, there will arise at the South such a minority, it will doubtless consist of men of religious and benevolent feelings,--men of that humane, and generous, and upright spirit, that most keenly feel the injuries inflicted on their fellow men. Suppose such a band of men begin their efforts, sustained by the northern Abolitionists, already so odious. How will the exasperated majority act, according to the known laws of mind and of experience? Instead of lessening the evils of slavery, they will increase them. The more they are goaded by a sense of aggressive wrong without, or by fears of dangers within, the more they will restrain their slaves, and diminish their liberty, and increase their disabilities. They will make laws so unjust and oppressive, not only to slaves, but to their Abolitionist advocates, that by degrees such men will withdraw from their bounds. Laws will be made expressly to harass them, and to render them so uncomfortable that they must withdraw. Then gradually the righteous will flee from the devoted city. Then the numerical proportion of whites will decrease, and the cruelty and unrestrained wickedness of the system will increase, till a period will come when the physical power will be so much with the blacks, their sense of suffering so increased, that the volcano will burst,--insurrection and servile wars will begin. Oh, the countless horrors of such a day! And will the South stand alone in that burning hour? When she sends forth the wailing of her agonies, shall not the North and the West hear, and lift up together the voice of wo? Will not fathers hear the cries of children, and brothers the cries of sisters? Will the terrors of insurrection sweep over the South, and no Northern and Western blood be shed? Will the slaves be cut down, in such a strife, when they raise the same paean song of liberty and human rights, that was the watchword of our redemption from far less dreadful tyranny, and which is now thrilling the nations and shaking monarchs on their thrones--will this be heard, and none of the sons of liberty be found to appear on their side? This is no picture of fancied dangers, which are not near. The day has come, when already the feelings are so excited on both sides, that I have heard intelligent men, good men, benevolent and pious men, in moments of excitement, declare themselves ready to take up the sword-- some for the defence of the master, some for the protection and right of the slave. It is my full conviction, that if insurrection does burst forth, and there be the least prospect of success to the cause of the slave, there will be men from the North and West, standing breast to breast, with murderous weapons, in opposing ranks.

Such apprehensions many would regard as needless, and exclaim against such melancholy predictions. But in a case where the whole point of duty and expediency turns upon the probabilities as to results, those probabilities ought to be the chief subjects of inquiry. True, no one has a right to say with confidence what will or what will not be; and it has often amazed and disturbed my mind to perceive how men, with so small a field of vision,--with so little data for judging,--with so few years, and so little experience, can pronounce concerning the results of measures bearing upon the complicated relations and duties of millions, and in a case where the wisest and best are dismayed and baffled. It sometimes has seemed to me that the prescience of Deity alone should dare to take such positions as are both carelessly assumed, and pertinaciously defended, by the advocates of Abolitionism.

But if we are to judge of the wisdom or folly of any measures on this subject, it must be with reference to future results. One course of measures, it is claimed, tends to perpetuate slavery, or to end it by scenes of terror and bloodshed. Another course tends to bring it to an end sooner, and by safe and peaceful influences. And the whole discussion of duty rests on these probabilities. But where do the laws of mind and experience oppose the terrific tendencies of Abolitionism that have been portrayed? Are not the minds of men thrown into a ferment, and excited by those passions which blind the reason, and warp the moral sense? Is not the South in a state of high exasperation against Abolitionists? Does she not regard them as enemies, as reckless madmen, as impertinent intermeddlers? Will the increase of their numbers tend to allay this exasperation? Will the appearance of a similar body in their own boundaries have any tendency to soothe? Will it not still more alarm and exasperate? If a movement of a minority of such men attempt to alter the laws, are not the probabilities strong that still more unjust and oppressive measures will be adopted?--measures that will tend to increase the hardships of the slave, and to drive out of the community all humane, conscientious and pious men? As the evils and dangers increase, will not the alarm constantly diminish the proportion of whites, and make it more and more needful to increase such disabilities and restraints as will chafe and inflame the blacks? When this point is reached, will the blacks, knowing, as they will know, the sympathies of their Abolition friends, refrain from exerting their physical power? ***The Southampton insurrection occurred with far less chance of sympathy and success.***

If that most horrible of all scourges, a servile war, breaks forth, will the slaughter of fathers, sons, infants, and of aged,--will the cries of wives, daughters, sisters, and kindred, suffering barbarities worse than death, bring no fathers, brothers, and friends to their aid, from the North and West?

And if the sympathies and indignation of freemen can already look such an event in the face, and feel that it would be the slave, rather than the master, whom they would defend, what will be the probability, after a few years' chafing shall have driven away the most christian and humane from scenes of cruelty and inhumanity, which they could neither alleviate nor redress? I should like to see any data of past experience, that will show that these results are not more probable than that the South will, by the system of means now urged upon her, finally be convinced of her sins, and voluntarily bring the system of slavery to an end. I claim not that the predictions I present will be fulfilled. I only say, that if Abolitionists go on as they propose, such results are *more* probable than those they hope to attain.

I have not here alluded to the probabilities of the severing of the Union by the present mode of agitating the question. This may be one of the results, and, if so, what are the probabilities for a Southern republic, that has torn itself off for the purpose of excluding foreign interference, and for the purpose of perpetuating slavery? Can any Abolitionist suppose that, in such a state of things, the great cause of emancipation is as likely to progress favourably, as it was when we were one nation, and mingling on those fraternal terms that existed before the Abolition movement began?

The preceding are some of the reasons which, on the general view, I would present as opposed to the proposal of forming Abolition Societies; and they apply equally to either sex. There are some others which seem to oppose peculiar objections to the action of females in the way you would urge.

To appreciate more fully these objections, it will be necessary to recur to some general views in relation to the place woman is appointed to fill by the dispensations of heaven.

It has of late become quite fashionable in all benevolent efforts, to shower upon our sex an abundance of compliments, not only for what they have done, but also for what they can do; and so injudicious and so frequent, are these oblations, that while I feel an increasing respect for my countrywomen, that their good sense has not been decoyed by these appeals to their vanity and ambition, I cannot but apprehend that there is some need of inquiry as to the just bounds of female influence, and the times, places, and manner in which it can be appropriately exerted.

It is the grand feature of the Divine economy, that there should be different stations of superiority and subordination, and it is impossible to annihilate this beneficent and immutable law. On its first entrance into life, the child is a dependent on parental love, and of necessity takes a place of subordination and obedience. As he advances in life these new relations of superiority and subordination multiply. The teacher must be the superior in station, the pupil a subordinate. The master of a family the superior, the domestic a subordinate--the ruler a superior, the subject a subordinate. Nor do these relations at all depend upon superiority either in intellectual or moral worth. However weak the parents, or intelligent the child, there is no reference to this, in the immutable law. However incompetent the teacher, or superior the pupil, no alteration of station can be allowed. However unworthy the master or worthy the servant, while their mutual relations continue, no change in station as to subordination can be allowed. In fulfilling the duties of these relations, true dignity consists in conforming to all those relations that demand subordination, with propriety and cheerfulness. When does a man, however high his character or station, appear more interesting or dignified than when yielding reverence and deferential attentions to an aged parent, however weak and infirm? And the pupil, the servant, or the subject, all equally sustain their own claims to self-respect, and to the esteem of others, by equally sustaining the appropriate relations and duties of subordination. In this arrangement of the duties of life, Heaven has appointed to one sex the superior, and to the other the subordinate station, and this without any reference to the character or conduct of either. It is therefore as much for the dignity as it is for the interest of females, in all respects to conform to the duties of this relation. And it is as much a duty as it is for the child to fulfil similar relations to parents, or subjects to rulers. But while woman holds a subordinate relation in society to the other sex, it is not because it was designed that her duties or her influence should be any the less important, or all-pervading. But it was designed that the mode of gaining influence and of exercising power should be altogether different and peculiar.

It is Christianity that has given to woman her true place in society. And it is the peculiar trait of Christianity alone that can sustain her therein. "Peace on earth and good will to men" is the character of all the rights and privileges, the influence, and the power of woman. A man may act on society by the collision of intellect, in public debate; he may urge his measures by a sense of shame, by fear and by personal interest; he may coerce by the combination of public sentiment; he may drive by physical force, and he does not outstep the boundaries of his sphere. But all the power, and all the conquests that are lawful to woman, are those only which appeal to the kindly, generous, peaceful and benevolent principles.

Woman is to win every thing by peace and love; by making herself so much respected, esteemed and loved, that to yield to her opinions and to gratify her wishes, will be the free-will offering of the heart. But this is to be all accomplished in the domestic and social circle. There let every woman become so cultivated and refined in intellect, that her taste and judgment will be respected; so benevolent in feeling and action, that her motives will be reverenced;--so unassuming and unambitious, that collision and competition will be banished;--so "gentle and easy to be entreated," as that every heart will repose in her presence; then, the fathers, the husbands, and the sons, will find an influence thrown around them, to which they will yield not only willingly but proudly. A man is never ashamed to own such influences, but feels dignified and ennobled in acknowledging them. But the moment woman begins to feel the promptings of ambition, or the thirst for power, her aegis of defence is gone. All the sacred protection of religion, all the generous promptings of chivalry, all the poetry of romantic gallantry, depend upon woman's retaining her place as dependent and defenceless, and making no claims, and maintaining no right but what are the gifts of honour, rectitude and love.

A woman may seek the aid of co-operation and combination among her own sex, to assist her in her appropriate offices of piety, charity, maternal and domestic duty; but whatever, in any measure, throws a woman into the attitude of a combatant, either for herself or others--whatever binds her in a party conflict--whatever obliges her in any way to exert coercive influences, throws her out of her appropriate sphere. If these general principles are correct, they are entirely opposed to the plan of arraying females in any Abolition movement; because it enlists them in an effort to coerce the South by the public sentiment of the North; because it brings them forward as partisans in a conflict that has been begun and carried forward by measures that are any thing rather than peaceful in their tendencies; because it draws them forth from their appropriate retirement, to expose themselves to the ungoverned violence of mobs, and to sneers and ridicule in public places; because it leads them into the arena of political collision, not as peaceful mediators to hush the opposing elements, but as combatants to cheer up and carry forward the measures of strife.

If it is asked, "May not woman appropriately come forward as a suppliant for a portion of her sex who are bound in cruel bondage?" It is replied, that, the rectitude and propriety of any such measure, depend entirely on its probable results. If petitions from females will operate to exasperate; if they will be deemed obtrusive, indecorous, and unwise, by those to whom they are addressed; if they will increase, rather than diminish the evil which it is wished to remove; if they will be the opening wedge, that will tend eventually to bring females as petitioners and partisans into every political measure that may tend to injure and oppress their sex, in various parts of the nation, and under the various public measures that may hereafter be enforced, then it is neither appropriate nor wise, nor right, for a woman to petition for the relief of oppressed females.

The case of Queen Esther is one often appealed to as a precedent. When a woman is placed in similar circumstances, where death to herself and all her nation is one alternative, and there is nothing worse to fear, but something to hope as the other alternative, then she may safely follow such an example. But when a woman is asked to join an Abolition Society, or to put her name to a petition to congress, for the purpose of contributing her measure of influence to keep up agitation in congress, to promote the excitement of the North against the iniquities of the South, to coerce the South by fear, shame, anger, and a sense of odium to do what she has determined not to do, the case of Queen Esther is not at all to be regarded as a suitable example for imitation.

In this country, petitions to congress, in reference to the official duties of legislators, seem, IN ALL CASES, to fall entirely without the sphere of female duty. Men are the proper persons to make appeals to the rulers whom they appoint, and if their female friends, by arguments and persuasions, can induce them to petition, all the good that can be done by such measures will be secured. But if females cannot influence their nearest friends, to urge forward a public measure in this way, they surely are out of their place, in attempting to do it themselves.

There are some other considerations, which should make the American females peculiarly sensitive in reference to any measure, which should even *seem* to draw them from their appropriate relations in society.

It is allowed by all reflecting minds, that the safety and happiness of this nation depends upon having the ***children*** educated, and not only intellectually, but morally and religiously. There are now nearly two millions of children and adults in this country who cannot read, and who have no schools of any kind. To give only a small supply of teachers to these destitute children, who are generally where the population is sparse, will demand *thirty thousand teachers*; and *six thousand* more will be needed every year, barely to meet the increase of juvenile population. But if we allow that we need not reach this point, in order to save ourselves from that destruction which awaits a people, when governed by an ignorant and unprincipled democracy; if we can weather the storms of democratic liberty with only one-third of our ignorant children properly educated, still we need *ten thousand* teachers at this moment, and an addition of *two thousand every year*. Where is this army of teachers to be found? Is it at all probable that the other sex will afford even a moderate portion of this supply? The field for enterprise and excitement in the political arena, in the arts, the sciences, the liberal professions, in agriculture, manufactures, and commerce, is opening with such temptations, as never yet bore upon the mind of any nation. Will men turn aside from these high and exciting objects to become the patient labourers in the school-room, and for only the small pittance that rewards such toil? No, they will not do it. Men will be educators in the college, in the high school, in some of the most honourable and lucrative common schools, but the ***children***, the ***little children*** of this nation must, to a wide extent, be taught by females, or remain untaught. The drudgery of education, as it is now too generally regarded, in this country, will be given to the female hand. And as the value of education rises in the public mind, and the importance of a teacher's office is more highly estimated, women will more and more be furnished with those intellectual advantages which they need to fit them for such duties.

The result will be, that America will be distinguished above all other nations, for well-educated females, and for the influence they will exert on the general interests of society. But if females, as they approach the other sex, in intellectual elevation, begin to claim, or to exercise in any manner, the peculiar prerogatives of that sex, education will prove a doubtful and dangerous blessing. But this will never be the result. For the more intelligent a woman becomes, the more she can appreciate the wisdom of that ordinance that appointed her subordinate station, and the more her taste will conform to the graceful and dignified retirement and submission it involves.

An ignorant, a narrow-minded, or a stupid woman, cannot feel nor understand the rationality, the propriety, or the beauty of this relation; and she it is, that will be most likely to carry her measures by tormenting, when she cannot please, or by petulant complaints or obtrusive interference, in matters which are out of her sphere, and which she cannot comprehend.

And experience testifies to this result. By the concession of all travellers, American females are distinguished above all others for their general intelligence, and yet they are complimented for their retiring modesty, virtue, and domestic faithfulness, while the other sex is as much distinguished for their respectful kindness and attentive gallantry. There is no other country where females have so much public respect and kindness accorded to them as in America, by the concession of all travellers. And it will ever be so, while intellectual culture in the female mind, is combined with the spirit of that religion which so strongly enforces the appropriate duties of a woman's sphere.

But it may be asked, is there nothing to be done to bring this national sin of slavery to an end? Must the internal slave-trade, a trade now ranked as piracy among all civilized nations, still prosper in our bounds? Must the very seat of our government stand as one of the chief slave-markets of the land; and must not Christian females open their lips, nor lift a finger, to bring such a shame and sin to an end?

To this it may be replied, that Christian females may, and can say and do much to bring these evils to an end; and the present is a time and an occasion when it seems most desirable that they should know, and appreciate, and ***exercise*** the power which they do possess for so desirable an end.

And in pointing out the methods of exerting female influence for this object, I am inspired with great confidence, from the conviction that what will be suggested, is that which none will oppose, but all will allow to be not only practicable, but safe, suitable, and Christian.

To appreciate these suggestions, however, it is needful previously to consider some particulars that exhibit the spirit of the age and the tendencies of our peculiar form of government.

The prominent principle, now in development, as indicating the spirit of the age, is the perfect right of all men to entire freedom of opinion. By this I do not mean that men are coming to think that "it is no matter what a man believes, if he is only honest and sincere," or that they are growing any more lenient towards their fellow-men, for the evil consequences they bring on themselves or on others for believing wrong.

But they are coming to adopt the maxim, that no man shall be forced by pains and penalties to adopt the opinions of other minds, but that every man shall be free to form his own opinions, and to propagate them by all lawful means.

At the same time another right is claimed, which is of necessity involved in the preceding,--the right to oppose, by all lawful means, the opinions and the practices of others, when they are deemed pernicious either to individuals or to the community. ***Facts***, ***arguments*** and ***persuasions*** are, by all, conceded to be lawful means to employ in propagating our own views, and in opposing the opinions and practices of others.

These fundamental principles of liberty have in all past ages been restrained by coercive influences, either of civil or of ecclesiastical power. But in this nation, all such coercive influences, both of church and state, have ceased. Every man may think what he pleases about government, or religion, or any thing else; he may propagate his opinions, he may controvert opposite opinions, and no magistrate or ecclesiastic can in any legal way restrain or punish.

But the form of our government is such, that every measure that bears upon the public or private interest of every citizen, is decided by ***public sentiment***. All laws and regulations in civil, or religious, or social concerns, are decided by the ***majority of votes***. And the present is a time when every doctrine, every principle, and every practice which influences the happiness of man, either in this, or in a future life, is under discussion. The whole nation is thrown into parties about almost every possible question, and every man is stimulated in his efforts to promote his own plans by the conviction that success depends entirely upon bringing his fellow citizens to think as he does. Hence every man is fierce in maintaining his own right of free discussion, his own right to propagate his opinions, and his own right to oppose, by all lawful means, the opinions that conflict with his own.

But the difficulty is, that a right which all men claim for themselves, with the most sensitive and pertinacious inflexibility, they have not yet learned to accord to their fellow men, in cases where their own interests are involved. Every man is saying, "Let me have full liberty to propagate my opinions, and to oppose all that I deem wrong and injurious, but let no man take this liberty with my opinions and practices. Every man may believe what he pleases, and propagate what he pleases, provided he takes care not to attack any thing which belongs to me."

And how do men exert themselves to restrain this corresponding right of their fellow men? Not by going to the magistrate to inform, or to the spiritual despot to obtain ecclesiastical penalties, but he resorts to methods, which, if successful, are in effect the most severe pains and penalties that can restrain freedom of opinion.

What is dearer to a man than ***his character***, involving as it does, the esteem, respect and affection of friends, neighbours and society, with all the confidence, honour, trust and emolument that flow from general esteem? How sensitive is every man to any thing that depreciates his intellectual character! What torture, to be ridiculed or pitied for such deficiencies! How cruel the suffering, when his moral delinquencies are held up to public scorn and reprehension! Confiscation, stripes, chains, and even death itself, are often less dreaded.

It is this method of punishment to which men resort, to deter their fellow-men from exercising those rights of liberty which they so tenaciously claim for themselves. Examine now the methods adopted by almost all who are engaged in the various conflicts of opinion in this nation, and you will find that there are certain measures which combatants almost invariably employ.

They either attack the intellectual character of opponents, or they labour to make them appear narrow-minded, illiberal and bigoted, or they impeach their honesty and veracity, or they stigmatize their motives as mean, selfish, ambitious, or in some other respect unworthy and degrading. Instead of truth, and evidence, and argument, personal depreciation, sneers, insinuations, or open abuse, are the weapons employed. This method of resisting freedom of opinions, by pains and penalties, arises in part from the natural selfishness of man, and in part from want of clear distinctions as to the rights and duties involved in freedom of opinion and freedom of speech.

The great fundamental principle that makes this matter clear, is this, that a broad and invariable distinction should ever be preserved between the ***opinions*** and ***practices*** that are discussed, and the ***advocates*** of these opinions and practices.

It is a sacred and imperious duty, that rests on every human being, to exert all his influence in opposing every thing that he believes is dangerous and wrong, and in sustaining all that he believes is safe and right. And in doing this, no compromise is to be made, in order to shield country, party, friends, or even self, from any just censure. Every man is bound by duty to God and to his country, to lay his finger on every false principle, or injurious practice, and boldly say, "this is wrong--this is dangerous--this I will oppose with all my influence, whoever it may be that advocates or practises it." And every man is bound to use his efforts to turn public sentiment against all that he believes to be wrong and injurious, either in regard to this life, or to the future world. And every man deserves to be respected and applauded, just in proportion as he fearlessly and impartially, and in a ***proper spirit***, ***time*** and ***manner***, fulfils this duty.

The doctrine, just now alluded to, that it is "no matter what a man believes, if he is only honest and sincere," is as pernicious, as it is contrary to religion and to common sense. It is as absurd, and as impracticable, as it would be to urge on the mariner the maxim, "no matter which way you believe to be north, if you only steer aright." A man's character, feelings, and conduct, all depend upon his opinions. If a man can reason himself into the belief that it is right to take the property of others and to deceive by false statements, he will probably prove a thief and a liar. It is of the greatest concern, therefore, to every man, that his fellow-men should ***believe right***, and one of his most sacred duties is to use all his influence to promote correct opinions.

But the performance of this duty, does by no means involve the necessity of attacking the character or motives of the ***advocates*** of false opinions, or of holding them up, individually, to public odium.

Erroneous opinions are sometimes the consequence of unavoidable ignorance, or of mental imbecility, or of a weak and erring judgment, or of false testimony from others, which cannot be rectified. In such cases, the advocates of false opinions are to be pitied rather than blamed; and while the opinions and their tendencies may be publicly exposed, the men may be objects of affection and kindness.

In other cases, erroneous opinions spring from criminal indifference, from prejudice, from indolence, from pride, from evil passions, or from selfish interest. In all such cases, men deserve blame for their pernicious opinions, and the evils which flow from them.

But, it maybe asked, how are men to decide, when their fellow-men are guilty for holding wrong opinions; when they deserve blame, and when they are to be regarded only with pity and commiseration by those who believe them to be in the wrong? Here, surely, is a place where some correct principle is greatly needed.

Is every man to sit in judgment upon his fellow-man, and decide what are his intellectual capacities, and what the measure of his judgment? Is every man to take the office of the Searcher of Hearts, to try the feelings and motives of his fellow-man? Is that most difficult of all analysis, the estimating of the feelings, purposes, and motives, which every man, who examines his own secret thoughts, finds to be so complex, so recondite, so intricate; is this to be the basis, not only of individual opinion, but of public reward and censure? Is every man to constitute himself a judge of the amount of time and interest given to the proper investigation of truth by his fellow-man? Surely, this cannot be a correct principle.

Though there may be single cases in which we can know that our fellow-men are weak in intellect, or erring in judgment, or perverse in feeling, or misled by passion, or biased by selfish interest, as a general fact we are not competent to decide these matters, in regard to those who differ from us in opinion.

For this reason it is manifestly wrong and irrelevant, when discussing questions of duty or expediency, to bring before the public the character or the motives of the individual advocates of opinions.

But, it may be urged, how can the evil tendencies of opinions or of practices be investigated, without involving a consideration of the character and conduct of those who advocate them? To this it may be replied, that the tendencies of opinions and practices can never be ascertained by discussing individual character. It is *classes* of persons, or large *communities*, embracing persons of all varieties of character and circumstances, that are the only proper subjects of investigation for this object. For example, a community of Catholics, and a community of Protestants, may be compared, for the purpose of learning the moral tendencies of their different opinions. Scotland and New England, where the principles opposite to Catholicism have most prevailed, may properly be compared with Spain and Italy, where the Catholic system has been most fairly tried. But to select certain individuals who are defenders of these two different systems, as examples to illustrate their tendencies, would be as improper as it would be to select a kernel of grain to prove the good or bad character of a whole crop.

To illustrate by a more particular example. The doctrines of the Atheist school are now under discussion, and Robert Owen and Fanny Wright have been their prominent advocates.

In agreement with the above principles, it is a right, and the duty of every man who has any influence and opportunity, to show the absurdity of their doctrines, the weakness of their arguments, and the fatal tendencies of their opinions. It is right to show that the *practical* adoption of their principles indicates a want of common sense, just as sowing the ocean with grain and expecting a crop would indicate the same deficiency. If the advocates of these doctrines carry out their principles into practice, in any such way as to offend the taste, or infringe on the rights of others, it is proper to express disgust and disapprobation. If the female advocate chooses to come upon a stage, and expose her person, dress, and elocution to public criticism, it is right to express disgust at whatever is offensive and indecorous, as it is to criticize the book of an author, or the dancing of an actress, or any thing else that is presented to public observation. And it is right to make all these things appear as odious and reprehensible to others as they do to ourselves.

But what is the private character of Robert Owen or Fanny Wright? Whether they are ignorant or weak in intellect; whether they have properly examined the sources of truth; how much they have been biased by pride, passion, or vice, in adopting their opinions; whether they are honest and sincere in their belief; whether they are selfish or benevolent in their aims, are not matters which in any way pertain to the discussion. They are questions about which none are qualified to judge, except those in close and intimate communion with them. We may inquire with propriety as to the character of a *community* of Atheists, or of a community where such sentiments extensively prevail, as compared with a community of opposite sentiments. But the private character, feelings, and motives of the individual advocates of these doctrines, are not proper subjects of investigation in any public discussion.

If, then, it be true, that attacks on the character and motives of the advocates of opinions are entirely irrelevant and not at all necessary for the discovery of truth; if injury inflicted on character is the most severe penalty that can be employed to restrain freedom of opinions and freedom of speech, what are we to say of the state of things in this nation?

Where is there a party which does not in effect say to every man, "if you dare to oppose the principles or practices we sustain, you shall be punished with personal odium?" which does not say to every member of the party, "uphold your party, right or wrong; oppose all that is adverse to your party, right or wrong, or else suffer the penalty of having your motives, character, and conduct, impeached?"

Look first at the political arena. Where is the advocate of any measure that does not suffer sneers, ridicule, contempt, and all that tends to depreciate character in public estimation? Where is the partisan that is not attacked, as either weak in intellect, or dishonest in principle, or selfish in motives? And where is the man who is linked with any political party, that dares to stand up fearlessly and defend what is good in opposers, and reprove what is wrong in his own party?

Look into the religious world. There, even those who take their party name from their professed liberality, are saying, "whoever shall adopt principles that exclude us from the Christian church, and our clergy from the pulpit, shall be held up either as intellectually degraded, or as narrow-minded and bigoted, or as ambitious, partisan and persecuting in spirit. No man shall believe a creed that excludes us from the pale of Christianity, under penalty of all the odium we can inflict."

So in the Catholic controversy. Catholics and their friends practically declare war against all free discussion on this point. The decree has gone forth, that "no man shall appear for the purpose of proving that Catholicism is contrary to Scripture, or immoral and anti-republican in tendency, under penalty of being denounced as a dupe, or a hypocrite, or a persecutor, or a narrow-minded and prejudiced bigot."

On the contrary, those who attack what is called liberal Christianity, or who aim to oppose the progress of Catholicism, how often do they exhibit a severe and uncharitable spirit towards the individuals whose opinions they controvert. Instead of loving the men, and rendering to them all the offices of Christian kindness, and according to them all due credit for whatever is desirable in character and conduct, how often do opposers seem to feel, that it will not answer to allow that there is any thing good, either in the system or in those who have adopted it. "Every thing about my party is right, and every thing in the opposing party is wrong," seems to be the universal maxim of the times. And it is the remark of some of the most intelligent foreign travellers among us, and of our own citizens who go abroad, that there is no country to be found, where freedom of opinion, and freedom of speech is more really influenced and controlled by the fear of pains and penalties, than in this land of boasted freedom. In other nations, the control is exercised by government, in respect to a very few matters; in this country it is party-spirit that rules with an iron rod, and shakes its scorpion whips over every interest and every employment of man.

From this mighty source spring constant detraction, gossiping, tale-bearing, falsehood, anger, pride, malice, revenge, and every evil word and work.

Every man sets himself up as the judge of the intellectual character, the honesty, the sincerity, the feelings, opportunities, motives, and intentions, of his fellow-man. And so they fall upon each other, not with swords and spears, but with the tongue, "that unruly member, that setteth on fire the course of nature, and is set on fire of hell."

Can any person who seeks to maintain the peaceful, loving, and gentle spirit of Christianity, go out into the world at this day, without being bewildered at the endless conflicts, and grieved and dismayed at the bitter and unhallowed passions they engender? Can an honest, upright and Christian man, go into these conflicts, and with unflinching firmness stand up for all that is good, and oppose all that is evil, in whatever party it may be found, without a measure of moral courage such as few can command? And if he carries himself through with an unyielding integrity, and maintains his consistency, is he not exposed to storms of bitter revilings, and to peltings from both parties between which he may stand?

What is the end of these things to be? Must we give up free discussion, and again chain up the human mind under the despotism of past ages? No, this will never be. God designs that every intelligent mind shall be governed, not by coercion, but by reason, and conscience, and truth. Man must reason, and experiment, and compare past and present results, and hear and know all that can be said on ***both*** sides of every question which influences either private or public happiness, either for this life or for the life to come.

But while this process is going on, must we be distracted and tortured by the baleful passions and wicked works that unrestrained party-spirit and ungoverned factions will bring upon us, under such a government as ours? Must we rush on to disunion, and civil wars, and servile wars, till all their train of horrors pass over us like devouring fire?

There is an influence that can avert these dangers--a spirit that can allay the storm--that can say to the troubled winds and waters, "peace, be still."

It is that spirit which is gentle and easy to be entreated, which thinketh no evil, which rejoiceth not in iniquity, but rejoiceth in the truth, which is not easily provoked, which hopeth all things, which beareth all things. Let this spirit be infused into the mass of the nation, and then truth may be sought, defended, and propagated, and error detected, and its evils exposed; and yet we may escape the evils that now rage through this nation, and threaten us with such fiery plagues.

And is there not a peculiar propriety in such an emergency, in looking for the especial agency and assistance of females, who are shut out from the many temptations that assail the other sex,--who are the appointed ministers of all the gentler charities of life,--who are mingled throughout the whole mass of the community,--who dwell in those retirements where only peace and love ought ever to enter,--whose comfort, influence, and dearest blessings, all depend on preserving peace and good will among men?

In the present aspect of affairs among us, when everything seems to be tending to disunion and distraction, it surely has become the duty of every female instantly to relinquish the attitude of a partisan, in every matter of clashing interests, and to assume the office of a mediator, and an advocate of peace. And to do this, it is not necessary that a woman should in any manner relinquish her opinion as to the evils or the benefits, the right or the wrong, of any principle or practice. But, while quietly holding her own opinions, and calmly avowing them, when conscience and integrity make the duty imperative, every female can employ her influence, not for the purpose of exciting or regulating public sentiment, but rather for the purpose of promoting a spirit of candour, forbearance, charity, and peace.

And there are certain prominent maxims which every woman can adopt as peculiarly belonging to her, as the advocate of charity and peace, and which it should be her especial office to illustrate, enforce, and sustain, by every method in her power.

The first is, that every person ought to be sustained, not only in the right of propagating his own opinions and practices, but in opposing all those principles and practices which he deems erroneous. For there is no opinion which a man can propagate, that does not oppose some adverse interest; and if a man must cease to advocate his own views of truth and rectitude, because he opposes the interest or prejudices of some other man or party, all freedom of opinion, of speech, and of action, is gone. All that can be demanded is, that a man shall not resort to falsehood, false reasoning, or to attacks on character, in maintaining his own rights. If he states things which are false, it is right to show the falsehood,--if he reasons falsely, it is right to point out his sophistry,--if he impeaches the character or motives of opponents, it is right to express disapprobation and disgust; but if he uses only facts, arguments, and persuasions, he is to be honoured and sustained for all the efforts he makes to uphold what he deems to be right, and to put down what he believes to be wrong.

Another maxim, which is partially involved in the first, is, that every man ought to allow his own principles and practices to be freely discussed, with patience and magnanimity, and not to complain of persecution, or to attack the character or motives of those who claim that he is in the wrong. If he is belied, if his character is impeached, if his motives are assailed, if his intellectual capabilities are made the objects of sneers or commiseration, he has a right to complain, and to seek sympathy as an injured man; but no man is a consistent friend and defender of liberty of speech, who cannot bear to have his own principles and practices subjected to the same ordeal as he demands should be imposed on others.

Another maxim of peace and charity is, that every man's own testimony is to be taken in regard to his motives, feelings, and intentions. Though we may fear that a fellow-man is mistaken in his views of his own feelings, or that he does not speak the truth, it is as contrary to the rules of good breeding as it is to the laws of Christianity, to assume or even insinuate that this is the case. If a man's word cannot be taken in regard to his own motives, feelings, and intentions, he can find no redress for the wrong that may be done to him. It is unjust and unreasonable in the extreme to take any other course than the one here urged.

Another most important maxim of candour and charity is, that when we are to assign motives for the conduct of our fellow-men, especially of those who oppose our interests, we are obligated to put the best, rather than the worst construction, on all they say and do. Instead of assigning the worst as the probable motive, it is always a duty to **hope** that it is the best, until evidence is so unequivocal that there is no place for such a hope.

Another maxim of peace and charity respects the subject of **retaliation**. Whatever may be said respecting the literal construction of some of the rules of the gospel, no one can deny that they do, whether figurative or not, forbid retaliation and revenge; that they do assume that men are not to be judges and executioners of their own wrongs; but that injuries are to be borne with meekness, and that retributive justice must be left to God, and to the laws. If a man strikes, we are not to return the blow, but appeal to the laws. If a man uses abusive or invidious language, we are not to return railing for railing. If a man impeaches our motives and attacks our character, we are not to return the evil. If a man sneers and ridicules, we are not to retaliate with ridicule and sneers. If a man reports our weaknesses and failings, we are not to revenge ourselves by reporting his. No man has a right to report evil of others, except when the justification of the innocent, or a regard for public or individual safety, demands it. This is the strict law of the gospel, inscribed in all its pages, and meeting in the face all those unchristian and indecent violations that now are so common, in almost every conflict of intellect or of interest.

Another most important maxim of peace and charity imposes the obligation to guard our fellow-men from all unnecessary temptation. We are taught daily to pray, "lead us not into temptation;" and thus are admonished not only to avoid all unnecessary temptation ourselves, but to save our fellow-men from the danger. Can we ask our Heavenly Parent to protect us from temptation, while we recklessly spread baits and snares for our fellow-men? No, we are bound in every measure to have a tender regard for the weaknesses and liabilities of all around, and ever to be ready to yield even our just rights, when we can lawfully do it, rather than to tempt others to sin. The generous and high-minded Apostle declares, "if meat make my brother to offend, I will eat no flesh while the world standeth;" and it is the spirit of this maxim that every Christian ought to cultivate. There are no occasions when this maxim is more needed, than when we wish to modify the opinions, or alter the practices of our fellow-men. If, in such cases, we find that the probabilities are, that any interference of ours will increase the power of temptation, and lead to greater evils than those we wish to remedy, we are bound to forbear. If we find that one mode of attempting a measure will increase the power of temptation, and another will not involve this danger, we are bound to take the safest course. In all cases we are obligated to be as careful to protect our fellow-men from temptation, as we are to watch and pray against it in regard to ourselves.

Another maxim of peace and charity requires a most scrupulous regard to the reputation, character, and feelings of our fellow-men, and especially of those who are opposed in any way to our wishes and interests. Every man and every woman feels that it is wrong for others to propagate their faults and weakness through the community. Every one feels wounded and injured to find that others are making his defects and infirmities the subject of sneers and ridicule. And what, then, is the rule of duty? "As ye would that men should do to you, do ye even so to them." With this rule before his eyes and in his mind, can a man retail his neighbour's faults, or sneer at his deficiencies, or ridicule his infirmities, with a clear conscience? There are cases when the safety of individuals, or public justice, demands that a man's defects of character, or crimes, be made public; but no man is justified in communicating to others any evil respecting any of his fellow-men, when he cannot appeal to God as his witness that he does it from benevolent interest in the welfare of his fellow-men--from a desire to save individuals or the public from some evil--and not from a malevolent or gossiping propensity. Oh, that this law of love and charity could find an illustration and an advocate in every female of this nation! Oh, that every current slander, and every injurious report, might stand abashed, whenever it meets the notice of a woman!

These are the maxims of peace and charity, which it is in the power of the females of our country to advocate, both by example and by entreaties. These are the principles which alone can protect and preserve the right of free discussion, the freedom of speech, and liberty of the press. And with our form of government, and our liabilities to faction and party-spirit, the country will be safe and happy only in proportion to the prevalence of these maxims among the mass of the community. There probably will never arrive a period in the history of this nation, when the influence of these principles will be more needed, than the present. The question of slavery involves more pecuniary interests, touches more private relations, involves more prejudices, is entwined with more sectional, party, and political interests, than any other which can ever again arise. It is a matter which, if discussed and controlled without the influence of these principles of charity and peace, will shake this nation like an earthquake, and pour over us the volcanic waves of every terrific passion. The trembling earth, the low murmuring thunders, already admonish us of our danger; and if females can exert any saving influence in this emergency, it is time for them to awake.

And there are topics that they may urge upon the attention of their friends, at least as matters worthy of serious consideration and inquiry.

Is a woman surrounded by those who favour the Abolition measures? Can she not with propriety urge such inquiries as these?

Is not slavery to be brought to an end by free discussion, and is it not a war upon the right of free discussion to impeach the motives and depreciate the character of the opposers of Abolition measures? When the opposers of Abolition movements claim that they honestly and sincerely believe that these measures tend to perpetuate slavery, or to bring it to an end by servile wars, and civil disunion, and the most terrific miseries--when they object to the use of their pulpits, to the embodying of literary students, to the agitation of the community, by Abolition agents--when they object to the circulation of such papers and tracts as Abolitionists prepare, because they believe them most pernicious in their influence and tendencies, is it not as much persecution to use invidious insinuations, depreciating accusation and impeachment of motive, in order to intimidate, as it is for the opposers of Abolitionism to use physical force? Is not the only method by which the South can be brought to relinquish slavery, a conviction that not only her ***duty***, but her highest ***interest***, requires her to do it? And is not ***calm, rational Christian*** discussion the only proper method of securing this end? Can a community that are thrown into such a state of high exasperation as now exists at the South, ever engage in such discussions, till the storm of excitement and passion is allayed? Ought not every friend of liberty and of free discussion, to take every possible means to soothe exasperated feelings, and to avoid all those offensive peculiarities that in their nature tend to inflame and offend?

Is a woman among those who oppose Abolition movements? She can urge such inquiries as these: Ought not Abolitionists to be treated as if they were actuated by the motives of benevolence which they profess? Ought not every patriot and every Christian to throw all his influence against the impeachment of motives, the personal detraction, and the violent measures that are turned upon this body of men, who, however they may err in judgment or in spirit, are among the most exemplary and benevolent in the land? If Abolitionists are censurable for taking measures that exasperate rather than convince and persuade, are not their opponents, who take exactly the same measures to exasperate Abolitionists and their friends, as much to blame? If Abolitionism prospers by the abuse of its advocates, are not the authors of this abuse accountable for the increase of the very evils they deprecate?

It is the opinion of intelligent and well informed men, that a very large proportion of the best members of the Abolition party were placed there, not by the arguments of Abolitionists, but by the abuse of their opposers. And I know some of the noblest minds that stand there, chiefly from the influence of those generous impulses that defend the injured and sustain the persecuted, while many others have joined these ranks from the impression that Abolitionism and the right of free discussion have become identical interests. Although I cannot perceive why the right of free discussion, the right of petition, and other rights that have become involved in this matter, cannot be sustained without joining an association that has sustained such injurious action and such erroneous principles, yet other minds, and those which are worthy of esteem, have been led to an opposite conclusion.

The South, in the moments of angry excitement, have made unreasonable demands upon the non-slave-holding States, and have employed overbearing and provoking language. This has provoked re-action again at the North, and men, who heretofore were unexcited, are beginning to feel indignant, and to say, "Let the Union be sundered." Thus anger begets anger, and unreasonable measures provoke equally unreasonable returns.

But when men, in moments of excitement rush on to such results, little do they think of the momentous consequences that may follow. Suppose the South in her anger unites with Texas, and forms a Southern slave-holding republic, under all the exasperating influences that such an avulsion will excite? What will be the prospects of the slave then, compared with what they are while we dwell together, united by all the ties of brotherhood, and having free access to those whom we wish to convince and persuade?

But who can estimate the mischiefs that we must encounter while this dismemberment, this tearing asunder of the joints and members of the body politic, is going on? What will be the commotion and dismay, when all our sources of wealth, prosperity, and comfort, are turned to occasions for angry and selfish strife?

What agitation will ensue in individual States, when it is to be decided by majorities which State shall go to the North and which to the South, and when the discontented minority must either give up or fight! Who shall divide our public lands between contending factions? What shall be done with our navy and all the various items of the nation's property? What shall be done when the post-office stops its steady movement to divide its efforts among contending parties? What shall be done when public credit staggers, when commerce furls her slackened sail, when property all over the nation changes its owners and relations? What shall be done with our canals and railways, now the bands of love to bind us, then the causes of contention and jealousy? What umpire will appear to settle all these questions of interest and strife, between communities thrown asunder by passion, pride, and mutual injury?

It is said that the American people, though heedless and sometimes reckless at the approach of danger, are endowed with a strong and latent principle of common sense, which, when they fairly approach the precipice, always brings them to a stand, and makes them as wise to devise a remedy as they were rash in hastening to the danger. Are we not approaching the very verge of the precipice? Can we not already hear the roar of the waters below? Is not now the time, if ever, when our stern principles and sound common sense must wake to the rescue?

Cannot the South be a little more patient under the injurious action that she feels she has suffered, and cease demanding those concessions from the North, that never will be made? For the North, though slower to manifest feeling, is as sensitive to her right of freedom of speech, as the South can be to her rights of property.

Cannot the North bear with some unreasonable action from the South, when it is remembered that, as the provocation came from the North, it is wise and Christian that the aggressive party should not so strictly hold their tempted brethren to the rules of right and reason?

Cannot the South bear in mind that at the North the colour of the skin does not take away the feeling of brotherhood, and though it is a badge of degradation in station and intellect, yet it is oftener regarded with pity and sympathy than with contempt? Cannot the South remember their generous feelings for the Greeks and Poles, and imagine that some such feelings may be awakened for the African race, among a people who do not believe either in the policy or the right of slavery?

Cannot the North remember how jealous every man feels of his domestic relations and rights, and how sorely their Southern brethren are tried in these respects? How would the husbands and fathers at the North endure it, if Southern associations should be formed to bring forth to the world the sins of Northern men, as husbands and fathers? What if the South should send to the North to collect all the sins and neglects of Northern husbands and fathers, to retail them at the South in tracts and periodicals? What if the English nation should join in the outcry, and English females should send forth an agent, not indeed to visit the offending North, but to circulate at the South, denouncing all who did not join in this crusade, as the defenders of bad husbands and bad fathers? How would Northern men conduct under such provocations? There is indeed a difference in the two cases, but it is not in the nature and amount of irritating influence, for the Southerner feels the interference of strangers to regulate his domestic duty to his servants, as much as the Northern man would feel the same interference in regard to his wife and children. Do not Northern men owe a debt of forbearance and sympathy toward their Southern brethren, who have been so sorely tried?

It is by urging these considerations, and by exhibiting and advocating the principles of charity and peace, that females may exert a wise and appropriate influence, and one which will most certainly tend to bring to an end, not only slavery, but unnumbered other evils and wrongs. No one can object to such an influence, but all parties will bid God speed to every woman who modestly, wisely and benevolently attempts it.

I do not suppose that any Abolitionists are to be deterred by any thing I can offer, from prosecuting the course of measures they have adopted. They doubtless will continue to agitate the subject, and to form voluntary associations all over the land, in order to excite public sentiment at the North against the moral evils existing at the South. Yet I cannot but hope that some considerations may have influence to modify in a degree the spirit and measures of some who are included in that party.

Abolitionists are men who come before the public in the character of **reprovers**. That the gospel requires Christians sometimes to assume this office, cannot be denied; but it does as unequivocally point out those qualifications which alone can entitle a man to do it. And no man acts wisely or consistently, unless he can satisfy himself that he possesses the qualifications for this duty, before he assumes it.

The first of these qualifications is more than common exemption from the faults that are reproved. The inspired interrogatory, "thou therefore which teachest another, teachest thou not thyself?" enforces this principle; and the maxim of common sense, that "reprovers must have clean hands," is no less unequivocal. Abolitionists are reprovers for the violation of duties in the domestic relations. Of course they are men who are especially bound to be exemplary in the discharge of all their domestic duties. If a man cannot govern his temper and his tongue; if he inflicts that moral castigation on those who cross his will, which is more severe than physical stripes; if he is overbearing or exacting with those under his control; if he cannot secure respect for a kind and faithful discharge of all his social and relative duties, it is as unwise and improper for him to join an Abolition Society, as it would be for a drunkard to preach temperance, or a slave-holder Abolitionism.

Another indispensable requisite for the office of reprover is a character distinguished for humility and meekness. There is nothing more difficult than to approach men for the purpose of convincing them of their own deficiencies and faults; and whoever attempts it in a self-complacent and dictatorial spirit, always does more evil than good. However exemplary a man may be in the sight of men, there is abundant cause for the exercise of humility. For a man is to judge of himself, not by a comparison with other men, but as he stands before God, when compared with a perfect law, and in reference to all his peculiar opportunities and restraints. Who is there that in this comparison, cannot find cause for the deepest humiliation? Who can go from the presence of Infinite Purity after such an investigation, to "take his brother by the throat?" Who rather, should not go to a brother, who may have sinned, with the deepest sympathy and love, as one who, amid greater temptations and with fewer advantages, may be the least offender of the two? A man who goes with this spirit, has the best hope of doing good to those who may offend. And yet even this spirit will not always save a man from angry retort, vexatious insinuation, jealous suspicion, and the misconstruction of his motives. A reprover, therefore, if he would avoid a quarrel and do the good he aims to secure, must be possessed of that meekness which can receive evil for good, with patient benevolence. And a man is not fitted for the duties of a reprover, until he can bring his feelings under this control.

The last, and not the least important requisite for a reprover, is ***discretion***. This is no where so much needed as in cases where the domestic relations are concerned, for here is the place above all others, where men are most sensitive and unreasonable. There are none who have more opportunities for learning this, than those who act as teachers, especially if they feel the responsibility of a Christian and a friend, in regard to the moral interests of pupils. A teacher who shares with parents the responsibilities of educating their children, whose efforts may all be rendered useless by parental influences at home; who feels an affectionate interest in both parent and child, is surely the one who might seem to have a right to seek, and a chance of success in seeking, some modifications of domestic influences. And yet teachers will probably testify, that it is a most discouraging task, and often as likely to result in jealous alienation and the loss of influence over both parent and child, as in any good. It is one of the greatest compliments that can be paid to the good sense and the good feeling of a parent to dare to attempt any such measure. This may show how much discretion, and tact, and delicacy, are needed by those who aim to rectify evils in the domestic relations of mankind.

The peculiar qualifications, then, which make it suitable for a man to be an Abolitionist are, an exemplary discharge of all the domestic duties; humility, meekness, delicacy, tact, and discretion, and these should especially be the distinctive traits of those who take the place of *leaders* in devising measures.

And in performing these difficult and self-denying duties, there are no men who need more carefully to study the character and imitate the example of the Redeemer of mankind. He, indeed, was the searcher of hearts, and those reproofs which were based on the perfect knowledge of "all that is in man," we may not imitate. But we may imitate him, where he with so much gentleness, patience, and pitying love, encountered the weakness, the rashness, the selfishness, the worldliness of men. When the young man came with such self-complacency to ask what more he could do, how kindly he was received, how gently convinced of his great deficiency! When fire would have been called from heaven by his angry followers, how forbearing the rebuke! When denied and forsaken with oaths and curses by one of his nearest friends, what was it but a look of pitying love that sent the disciple out so bitterly to weep? When, in his last extremity of sorrow, his friends all fell asleep, how gently he drew over them the mantle of love! Oh blessed Saviour, impart more of thy own spirit to those who profess to follow thee!

www.bookjungle.com *email: sales@bookjungle.com fax: 630-214-0564 mail: Book Jungle PO Box 2226 Champaign, IL 61825*

### The Codes Of Hammurabi And Moses
### W. W. Davies

QTY

The discovery of the Hammurabi Code is one of the greatest achievements of archaeology, and is of paramount interest, not only to the student of the Bible, but also to all those interested in ancient history...

**Religion**   ISBN: *1-59462-338-4*   Pages:132
MSRP *$12.95*

### The Theory of Moral Sentiments
### Adam Smith

QTY

This work from 1749. contains original theories of conscience amd moral judgment and it is the foundation for systemof morals.

**Philosophy**   ISBN: *1-59462-777-0*   Pages:536
MSRP *$19.95*

### Jessica's First Prayer
### Hesba Stretton

QTY

In a screened and secluded corner of one of the many railway-bridges which span the streets of London there could be seen a few years ago, from five o'clock every morning until half past eight, a tidily set-out coffee-stall, consisting of a trestle and board, upon which stood two large tin cans, with a small fire of charcoal burning under each so as to keep the coffee boiling during the early hours of the morning when the work-people were thronging into the city on their way to their daily toil...

**Childrens**   ISBN: *1-59462-373-2*   Pages:84
MSRP *$9.95*

### My Life and Work
### Henry Ford

QTY

Henry Ford revolutionized the world with his implementation of mass production for the Model T automobile. Gain valuable business insight into his life and work with his own auto-biography... "We have only started on our development of our country we have not as yet, with all our talk of wonderful progress, done more than scratch the surface. The progress has been wonderful enough but..."

**Biographies/**   ISBN: *1-59462-198-5*   Pages:300
MSRP *$21.95*

www.bookjungle.com  *email: sales@bookjungle.com fax: 630-214-0564 mail: Book Jungle PO Box 2226 Champaign, IL 61825*

### The Art of Cross-Examination
### Francis Wellman

QTY

I presume it is the experience of every author, after his first book is published upon an important subject, to be almost overwhelmed with a wealth of ideas and illustrations which could readily have been included in his book, and which to his own mind, at least, seem to make a second edition inevitable. Such certainly was the case with me; and when the first edition had reached its sixth impression in five months, I rejoiced to learn that it seemed to my publishers that the book had met with a sufficiently favorable reception to justify a second and considerably enlarged edition. ..

Reference    ISBN: *1-59462-647-2*

Pages:412
MSRP *$19.95*

### On the Duty of Civil Disobedience
### Henry David Thoreau

QTY

Thoreau wrote his famous essay, On the Duty of Civil Disobedience, as a protest against an unjust but popular war and the immoral but popular institution of slave-owning. He did more than write—he declined to pay his taxes, and was hauled off to gaol in consequence. Who can say how much this refusal of his hastened the end of the war and of slavery ?

Law         ISBN: *1-59462-747-9*

Pages:48
MSRP *$7.45*

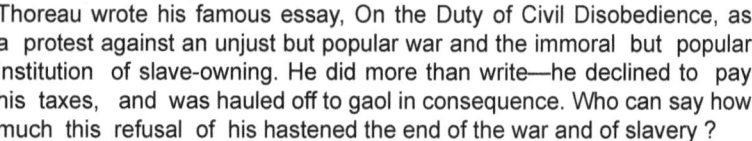

### Dream Psychology Psychoanalysis for Beginners
### Sigmund Freud

QTY

Sigmund Freud, born Sigismund Schlomo Freud (May 6, 1856 - September 23, 1939), was a Jewish-Austrian neurologist and psychiatrist who co-founded the psychoanalytic school of psychology. Freud is best known for his theories of the unconscious mind, especially involving the mechanism of repression; his redefinition of sexual desire as mobile and directed towards a wide variety of objects; and his therapeutic techniques, especially his understanding of transference in the therapeutic relationship and the presumed value of dreams as sources of insight into unconscious desires.

Psychology    ISBN: *1-59462-905-6*

Pages:196
MSRP *$15.45*

### The Miracle of Right Thought
### Orison Swett Marden

QTY

Believe with all of your heart that you will do what you were made to do. When the mind has once formed the habit of holding cheerful, happy, prosperous pictures, it will not be easy to form the opposite habit. It does not matter how improbable or how far away this realization may see, or how dark the prospects may be, if we visualize them as best we can, as vividly as possible, hold tenaciously to them and vigorously struggle to attain them, they will gradually become actualized, realized in the life. But a desire, a longing without endeavor, a yearning abandoned or held indifferently will vanish without realization.

Self Help       ISBN: *1-59462-644-8*

Pages:360
MSRP *$25.45*

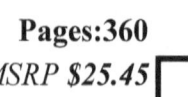

www.bookjungle.com  email: sales@bookjungle.com  fax: 630-214-0564  mail: Book Jungle  PO Box 2226  Champaign, IL 61825

QTY

| | Title | ISBN | Price |
|---|---|---|---|
| ☐ | **The Rosicrucian Cosmo-Conception Mystic Christianity** by *Max Heindel* | ISBN: 1-59462-188-8 | $38.95 |
| | The Rosicrucian Cosmo-conception is not dogmatic, neither does it appeal to any other authority than the reason of the student. It is: not controversial, but is: sent forth in the, hope that it may help to clear... | New Age/Religion Pages 646 | |
| ☐ | **Abandonment To Divine Providence** by *Jean-Pierre de Caussade* | ISBN: 1-59462-228-0 | $25.95 |
| | "The Rev. Jean Pierre de Caussade was one of the most remarkable spiritual writers of the Society of Jesus in France in the 18th Century. His death took place at Toulouse in 1751. His works have gone through many editions and have been republished... | Inspirational/Religion Pages 400 | |
| ☐ | **Mental Chemistry** by *Charles Haanel* | ISBN: 1-59462-192-6 | $23.95 |
| | Mental Chemistry allows the change of material conditions by combining and appropriately utilizing the power of the mind. Much like applied chemistry creates something new and unique out of careful combinations of chemicals the mastery of mental chemistry... | New Age Pages 354 | |
| ☐ | **The Letters of Robert Browning and Elizabeth Barret Barrett 1845-1846 vol II** by *Robert Browning and Elizabeth Barrett* | ISBN: 1-59462-193-4 | $35.95 |
| | | Biographies Pages 596 | |
| ☐ | **Gleanings In Genesis (volume I)** by *Arthur W. Pink* | ISBN: 1-59462-130-6 | $27.45 |
| | Appropriately has Genesis been termed "the seed plot of the Bible" for in it we have, in germ form, almost all of the great doctrines which are afterwards fully developed in the books of Scripture which follow... | Religion/Inspirational Pages 420 | |
| ☐ | **The Master Key** by *L. W. de Laurence* | ISBN: 1-59462-001-6 | $30.95 |
| | In no branch of human knowledge has there been a more lively increase of the spirit of research during the past few years than in the study of Psychology, Concentration and Mental Discipline. The requests for authentic lessons in Thought Control, Mental Discipline and... | New Age/Business Pages 422 | |
| ☐ | **The Lesser Key Of Solomon Goetia** by *L. W. de Laurence* | ISBN: 1-59462-092-X | $9.95 |
| | This translation of the first book of the "Lerngton" which is now for the first time made accessible to students of Talismanic Magic was done, after careful collation and edition, from numerous Ancient Manuscripts in Hebrew, Latin, and French... | New Age/Occult Pages 92 | |
| ☐ | **Rubaiyat Of Omar Khayyam** by *Edward Fitzgerald* | ISBN:1-59462-332-5 | $13.95 |
| | Edward Fitzgerald, whom the world has already learned, in spite of his own efforts to remain within the shadow of anonymity, to look upon as one of the rarest poets of the century, was born at Bredfield, in Suffolk, on the 31st of March, 1809. He was the third son of John Purcell... | Music Pages 172 | |
| ☐ | **Ancient Law** by *Henry Maine* | ISBN: 1-59462-128-4 | $29.95 |
| | The chief object of the following pages is to indicate some of the earliest ideas of mankind, as they are reflected in Ancient Law, and to point out the relation of those ideas to modern thought. | Religion/History Pages 452 | |
| ☐ | **Far-Away Stories** by *William J. Locke* | ISBN: 1-59462-129-2 | $19.45 |
| | "Good wine needs no bush, but a collection of mixed vintages does. And this book is just such a collection. Some of the stories I do not want to remain buried for ever in the museum files of dead magazine-numbers an author's not unpardonable vanity..." | Fiction Pages 272 | |
| ☐ | **Life of David Crockett** by *David Crockett* | ISBN: 1-59462-250-7 | $27.45 |
| | "Colonel David Crockett was one of the most remarkable men of the times in which he lived. Born in humble life, but gifted with a strong will, an indomitable courage, and unremitting perseverance... | Biographies/New Age Pages 424 | |
| ☐ | **Lip-Reading** by *Edward Nitchie* | ISBN: 1-59462-206-X | $25.95 |
| | Edward B. Nitchie, founder of the New York School for the Hard of Hearing, now the Nitchie School of Lip-Reading, Inc, wrote "LIP-READING Principles and Practice". The development and perfecting of this meritorious work on lip-reading was an undertaking... | How-to Pages 400 | |
| ☐ | **A Handbook of Suggestive Therapeutics, Applied Hypnotism, Psychic Science** by *Henry Munro* | ISBN: 1-59462-214-0 | $24.95 |
| | | Health/New Age/Health/Self-help Pages 376 | |
| ☐ | **A Doll's House: and Two Other Plays** by *Henrik Ibsen* | ISBN: 1-59462-112-8 | $19.95 |
| | Henrik Ibsen created this classic when in revolutionary 1848 Rome. Introducing some striking concepts in playwriting for the realist genre, this play has been studied the world over. | Fiction/Classics/Plays 308 | |
| ☐ | **The Light of Asia** by *sir Edwin Arnold* | ISBN: 1-59462-204-3 | $13.95 |
| | In this poetic masterpiece, Edwin Arnold describes the life and teachings of Buddha. The man who was to become known as Buddha to the world was born as Prince Gautama of India but he rejected the worldly riches and abandoned the reigns of power when... | Religion/History/Biographies Pages 170 | |
| ☐ | **The Complete Works of Guy de Maupassant** by *Guy de Maupassant* | ISBN: 1-59462-157-8 | $16.95 |
| | "For days and days, nights and nights, I had dreamed of that first kiss which was to consecrate our engagement, and I knew not on what spot I should put my lips..." | Fiction/Classics Pages 240 | |
| ☐ | **The Art of Cross-Examination** by *Francis L. Wellman* | ISBN: 1-59462-309-0 | $26.95 |
| | Written by a renowned trial lawyer, Wellman imparts his experience and uses case studies to explain how to use psychology to extract desired information through questioning. | How-to/Science/Reference Pages 408 | |
| ☐ | **Answered or Unanswered?** by *Louisa Vaughan* | ISBN: 1-59462-248-5 | $10.95 |
| | Miracles of Faith in China | Religion Pages 112 | |
| ☐ | **The Edinburgh Lectures on Mental Science (1909)** by *Thomas* | ISBN: 1-59462-008-3 | $11.95 |
| | This book contains the substance of a course of lectures recently given by the writer in the Queen Street Hall, Edinburgh. Its purpose is to indicate the Natural Principles governing the relation between Mental Action and Material Conditions... | New Age/Psychology Pages 148 | |
| ☐ | **Ayesha** by *H. Rider Haggard* | ISBN: 1-59462-301-5 | $24.95 |
| | Verily and indeed it is the unexpected that happens! Probably if there was one person upon the earth from whom the Editor of this, and of a certain previous history, did not expect to hear again... | Classics Pages 380 | |
| ☐ | **Ayala's Angel** by *Anthony Trollope* | ISBN: 1-59462-352-X | $29.95 |
| | The two girls were both pretty, but Lucy who was twenty-one who supposed to be simple and comparatively unattractive, whereas Ayala was credited, as her Bombwhat romantic name might show, with poetic charm and a taste for romance. Ayala when her father died was nineteen... | Fiction Pages 484 | |
| ☐ | **The American Commonwealth** by *James Bryce* | ISBN: 1-59462-286-8 | $34.45 |
| | An interpretation of American democratic political theory. It examines political mechanics and society from the perspective of Scotsman James Bryce | Politics Pages 572 | |
| ☐ | **Stories of the Pilgrims** by *Margaret P. Pumphrey* | ISBN: 1-59462-116-1 | $17.95 |
| | This book explores pilgrims religious oppression in England as well as their escape to Holland and eventual crossing to America on the Mayflower, and their early days in New England... | History Pages 268 | |

www.bookjungle.com *email:* sales@bookjungle.com *fax:* 630-214-0564 *mail:* Book Jungle  PO Box 2226  Champaign, IL 61825

| | | QTY |
|---|---|---|
| **The Fasting Cure** *by Sinclair Upton*<br>In the Cosmopolitan Magazine for May, 1910, and in the Contemporary Review (London) for April, 1910, I published an article dealing with my experiences in fasting. I have written a great many magazine articles, but never one which attracted so much attention... | **ISBN:** *1-59462-222-1*  **$13.95**<br>New Age/Self Help/Health Pages 164 | ☐ |
| **Hebrew Astrology** *by Sepharial*<br>In these days of advanced thinking it is a matter of common observation that we have left many of the old landmarks behind and that we are now pressing forward to greater heights and to a wider horizon than that which represented the mind-content of our progenitors... | **ISBN:** *1-59462-308-2*  **$13.45**<br>Astrology Pages 144 | ☐ |
| **Thought Vibration or The Law of Attraction in the Thought World**<br>*by William Walker Atkinson* | **ISBN:** *1-59462-127-6*  **$12.95**<br>Psychology/Religion Pages 144 | ☐ |
| **Optimism** *by Helen Keller*<br>Helen Keller was blind, deaf, and mute since 19 months old, yet famously learned how to overcome these handicaps, communicate with the world, and spread her lectures promoting optimism.  An inspiring read for everyone... | **ISBN:** *1-59462-108-X*  **$15.95**<br>Biographies/Inspirational Pages 84 | ☐ |
| **Sara Crewe** *by Frances Burnett*<br>In the first place, Miss Minchin lived in London. Her home was a large, dull, tall one, in a large, dull square, where all the houses were alike, and all the sparrows were alike, and where all the door-knockers made the same heavy sound... | **ISBN:** *1-59462-360-0*  **$9.45**<br>Childrens/Classic Pages 88 | ☐ |
| **The Autobiography of Benjamin Franklin** *by Benjamin Franklin*<br>The Autobiography of Benjamin Franklin has probably been more extensively read than any other American historical work, and no other book of its kind has had such ups and downs of fortune. Franklin lived for many years in England, where he was agent... | **ISBN:** *1-59462-135-7*  **$24.95**<br>Biographies/History Pages 332 | ☐ |

| | |
|---|---|
| **Name** | |
| **Email** | |
| **Telephone** | |
| **Address** | |
| | |
| **City, State ZIP** | |

☐ Credit Card     ☐ Check / Money Order

| | |
|---|---|
| **Credit Card Number** | |
| **Expiration Date** | |
| **Signature** | |

*Please Mail to:*   Book Jungle
                   PO Box 2226
                   Champaign, IL 61825
*or Fax to:*       630-214-0564

### ORDERING INFORMATION

**web**: www.bookjungle.com
**email**: sales@bookjungle.com
**fax**: 630-214-0564
**mail**: Book Jungle  PO Box 2226  Champaign, IL 61825
**or PayPal** *to* sales@bookjungle.com

*Please contact us for bulk discounts*

### DIRECT-ORDER TERMS

**20% Discount if You Order
Two or More Books**
Free Domestic Shipping!
Accepted: Master Card, Visa,
Discover, American Express